Monetarism, Economic Crisis and the Third World

Monetarism, Economic Crisis and the Third World

Edited by
KAREL JANSEN
Institute of Social Studies, The Hague

Frank Cass

First Published 1983 in Great Britain by
FRANK CASS AND COMPANY LIMITED
Gainsborough House, 11 Gainsborough Road,
London E11 1RS, England

and in the United States of America by
FRANK CASS AND COMPANY LIMITED
c/o Biblio Distribution Centre
81 Adams Drive, P.O. Box 327, Totowa, N.J. 07511.

Copyright © 1983 The Institute of Social Studies, The Hague

British Library Cataloguing in Publication Data

Jansen, Karel
    Monetarism, economic crisis and the Third
    World.
    1. Underdeveloped areas – Economic policy
    I. Title
    330.9172′4   HC59.7

    ISBN 0-7146-3222-8
    ISBN 0-7146-4037-9 Pbk

Typeset by John Smith, London
Printed and Bound in Great Britain by
Robert Hartnoll Ltd. Bodmin, Cornwall

Contents

Foreword   *Louis Emmerij*   vii

Preface   *Karel Jansen*   ix

About the Contributors   xi

  I Monetarism, Economic Crisis and the Third
     World: An Introduction   1
     Karel Jansen

 II The Origins and Evolution of Monetarism   43
     Robert Mundell

III What is Wrong with Monetarism?   55
     Francis Cripps

 IV Monetarism: Is the Debate Closed?   69
     Arnold Heertje

  V World Crisis and the Monetarist Answer   79
     Ernest Mandel

 VI Monetarism and the State Socialist World   96
     Michael Ellman

Contents

VII Structuralism vs Monetarism in Latin America:
A Reappraisal of a Great Debate, with Lessons
for Europe in the 1980s   110

Dudley Seers

VIII The IMF Prescription for Structural
Adjustment in Tanzania   127

Brian Van Arkadie

IX International Keynesianism – A Solution to the
World Crisis?   149

Lal Jayawardena

X Monetarist Policies on a World Scale   175

Jacques Polak

Index   189

Foreword

We are faced in the industrialised countries with at least four competing economic philosophies: Keynesianism or post-Keynesianism, monetarism, supply-side economics, and the rational expectations school. This confusion reflects the embarrassing fact that policy makers and social scientists are unable to agree on their diagnosis of the present world economic situation, let alone on the medicine with which to cure our problems and to get the OECD economies moving again after a decade of economic recession and even depression.

The less rich and the poor countries have little choice but to adjust themselves to the bewilderment of policies (or lack of them caused by the *embarras du choix*) which unfolds in the North. Rather than working on a New International Economic Order, which is an attempt by the international order to adjust to the needs and problems of developing countries, the latter are expected to adjust to the existing order.

The unimaginative nature of the economic and social policies of the industrialised countries is equally striking. Indeed, two policies seem to be common: (i) the passive acceptance of low, zero, or even negative rates of economic growth, and (ii) the equally passive adjustment of the welfare state, which has been constructed during the last few decades, to this very low or even negative growth rate. The result is inevitably a downward spiral of economic activity.

A shift towards a far more active policy is needed – one which should include a programme of economic restructuring, a programme for the stimulation of international demand, and also, in all probability, monetary policies in the narrow sense of the word. I am happy to note that some contributors to this book give a good deal of consideration to the matter of international demand. It is an absurdity that the economic depression makes it impossible for part of our productive capacity, both human and physical, to be used while hundreds of millions of people in all parts of the world have to go without the most basic necessities which would enable them to lead a reasonable existence.

The work of the Institute of Social Studies focuses mainly on problems of the Third World seen in a global perspective, and it thus has a special interest in the theme of 'Monetarism, Economic Crisis and the Third World'. In fact, we have an obligation to take the monetarist debate out of its present confinement to First World problems, to place it in a world-wide perspective, and in particular to derive implications for the Third World.

To examine the problem of international finance and monetarism in a world perspective with emphasis on the developing countries is a neglected area of research. The Institute of Social Studies has started an ambitious research programme in this area, of which this volume is one of the first tangible results.

I wish to thank my colleague Karel Jansen for the tremendous amount of work that he has put into this volume. The result is an exceptionally rich and complete treatment of the topic.

Louis Emmerij
Rector
Institute of Social Studies

The Hague
October 1982

Preface

The papers collected in this book are based on the Public Lecture Series given at the Institute of Social Studies, The Hague, in 1982. When I was asked to organise that series on the theme 'Monetarism, Economic Crisis and the Third World', I looked upon it as an opportunity to draw the discussion on monetarist economic policies out of the restricted arena of current problems of the industrialised countries. Three aspects may be emphasised. First, the long-standing experience with monetarist policies in other parts of the world from which lessons can be drawn. Second, the current recession in, and the monetarist policies of, the industrialised countries have severe implications for the rest of the world. And third, the problems of the industrialised countries are to a large extent problems of the world economic system for which international solutions should be formulated. These three aspects appear in varying forms in the contributions to this book.

The authors of the papers have been so kind as to revise and edit their lecture notes to make them suitable for publication. I wish to thank them all for accepting the Institute's invitation to participate in the lecture series, and for further cooperating in the preparation of this book. My Introduction has been written specifically for the book and did not form part of the lecture series.

At the Institute, I must thank my colleagues Richard Brown, who launched the idea for a lecture series on this topic, Charles Cooper and Valpy FitzGerald for their support in the organisation of the lectures and in the preparation of this publication. I also thank the Rector of the Institute, Professor

Preface

Louis Emmerij, for his Foreword to the book, and Jean Sanders for an excellent job of copy-editing.

The Hague   Karel Jansen
October 1982

About the Contributors

Francis Cripps is Senior Research Officer, Department of Applied Economics, Cambridge, UK and a leading member of the Cambridge Economic Policy Group. He has been author and co-author of many works on economic policy in the United Kingdom, as well as on models of the world economy and of the European economy.

Michael Ellman is Professor in the Economic Theory of Centrally Planned Economies, University of Amsterdam. Previously, he was Research Officer at the Department of Applied Economics in Cambridge, and before that Lecturer at the University of Glasgow. He has written a book on Socialist Planning and numerous articles on economic policy in Eastern European countries and in China.

Arnold Heertje is Professor of Economics at the University of Amsterdam, and has written an important book on Economics and Technical Change. His basic textbooks in economics have been translated into many languages. He has also published widely on economic policy in the Netherlands.

Karel Jansen is Senior Lecturer in Economics at the Institute of Social Studies, The Hague, which he joined in 1975 after working for some years in Asia as an Educational Planner with UNESCO. He coordinates a Research Programme on Money, Finance and Development, and designed and organised at ISS the Public Lecture Series on which this book is based. He has published on economic policy and on the economic role of the state in developing countries.

About the Contributors

Lal Jayawardena at the time of writing was Ambassador of Sri Lanka to Belgium, the Netherlands and the EEC. Previously he had been Permanent Secretary of the Ministry of Finance and Planning in Sri Lanka. He is a very active participant in various Third World fora and international negotiations, such as the Group of 77; is Chairman of the group of 24 developing countries preparing proposals for reform of the IMF; and was Consultant to the Brandt Commission.

Ernest Mandel is Professor at the Free University in Brussels. A leading representative of the Marxist tradition in economics, he has written such books as *Late Capitalism, The Second Slump*, and *Long Waves of Capitalist Development; the Marxist Interpretation*. He is an active militant in the Fourth International.

Robert Mundell is Professor of Economics at Columbia University, New York, and was previously at the University of Chicago. His two principal books, *International Economics* (1968) and *Monetary Theory* (1971), constituted a theoretical basis for economic policy in an open economy, and provided the foundation for the monetary approach to the balance of payments. More recently he has been one of the leading forces behind supply-side economics.

Jacques Polak is Executive Director of the IMF. He has previously been a member of the Economic Secretariat of the League of Nations and Dutch Delegation member to the Bretton Woods Conference. He joined the IMF in 1947 and was Director of its Research Department until in 1980 he was elected Executive Director. He has written a series of articles that founded the IMF's view on the monetary approach to the balance of payments, a model which still forms the philosophy behind the IMF's conditionality policy.

Dudley Seers is Professorial Fellow at the Institute of Development Studies, University of Sussex. In the late 1950s he was with the Economic Commission of Latin America (ECLA), where he was one of the architects of the structuralist approach. Via Yale University, Economic Commission of Africa and British Government service, he went to the IDS of which he was Director for five years. He has been advisor to many Third World Governments and leader of the influential ILO World Employment Programme missions to Colombia and Sri Lanka. He has published widely, including on inflation in Latin America.

Brian Van Arkadie is Professor Extraordinary of Development Economics, Institute of Social Studies, The Hague and was previously Fellow of Queen's College, Cambridge and Director of that University's Centre for Latin American Studies. He was Advisor to the Tanzanian Ministry of Planning from 1966 to 1969, and went back in 1978 to co-author a report for UNCTAD on the adjustment to balance of payment shocks in Tanzania. In 1982 he served as Head of the Secretariat of an Advisory Group to the Tanzanian Government on Structural Adjustment.

1

Monetarism, Economic Crisis and the Third World: An Introduction

by KAREL JANSEN

INTRODUCTION

This book is about monetarism as an economic policy, and has two original features which distinguish it from the many other books on the subject. First and foremost, the economic problems of the 1970s which gave rise to the current popularity of monetarist policies are analysed on a world scale. Rich and poor countries in the capitalist and socialist worlds are affected by the current recession and monetarist policies have been introduced in many of them. In the contributions to this book the desirability and feasibility of monetarist policies in rich as well as in poor countries are discussed. Some contributors claim that the international nature of the current economic crisis requires an internationally-coordinated policy response.

The second outstanding feature of this book is that it brings together different and sometimes diametrically opposed theoretical and ideological positions, ranging from monetarism to post-Keynesianism, Structuralism and Marxism, a range that enables us to observe sometimes surprising agreement among those thought to be far apart, as well as sharp differences of opinion among those who are theoretically close. In general, the contributors show a fair degree of agreement in interpreting the nature of the current recession, but have sharp differences on the most appropriate policy to be followed. The resulting de-

I wish to thank my colleagues Charles Cooper and Valpy FitzGerald for many useful comments made on an earlier draft of this paper.

1

bate on economic policy in its world-wide perspective forms the substance of the book.

The economic recession of the 1970s and early 1980s affected all countries in the world but in different ways. What for industrial countries is a crisis of inflation and unemployment is for most developing countries a crisis of the balance of payments, and for some centrally-planned economies a crisis of high interest rates on external debts. Again, some developing countries have been able to weather the crisis remarkably well, maintaining growth rates far in excess of those of other countries, whether industrial or developing. The great majority of poor developing countries, however, have seen their export earnings stagnate and their development efforts frustrated.

Behind these obvious manifestations, in both industrialised and developing countries, more fundamental processes should be identified. In the industrial countries, longer-term trends of decelerated growth in labour productivity, of increasing relative size of the public sector, and of increasing rigidities in the operation of the labour markets, have resulted in declining profit shares, in accelerated inflation, and in increased unemployment. The oil price increases of 1973 and 1979 were the external shocks which pushed the already weakened economies into recession.

In contrast, the oil price increases and the subsequent recession in industrial countries constituted external shocks for the developing countries which were not new in nature – the primary commodities exporting countries are quite used to fluctuations in their export earnings – but were unique in their suddenness and extent. These shocks made it clear that the inward-looking policies followed by many developing countries had not reduced their import dependency or their vulnerability. To the contrary, in fact. The crisis thus raised again for the developing countries the problem of the most appropriate way in which to integrate with the world economy.

Although the economic crisis is experienced in various ways in different parts of the world, the proposed policy response has been more uniformly monetarist. The contributors to this book focus their analyses on monetarism as an economic policy rather than as an economic theory. They discuss whether a monetarist-inspired economic policy can contribute to the solution of economic problems at the national level in various parts of the world, as well as at the international level.

In today's world economy, with its highly integrated and internationalised commodities and capital markets, the autonomy and effectiveness of national economic policy is restricted. Hence the need, argued in several contributions to this book, for internationally-coordinated policy actions. Other contributors are less convinced of the feasibility of such international action and continue to concentrate on national policy making. The effectiveness of national policy can only be analysed in an international context, however, because the actions of one country have economic effects on others, and the success of an economic policy in an open economy is dependent on conditions and policies in others.

It is not surprising that the authors in this book, with their varied ideological and theoretical positions, and dealing with experiences of countries in the First, Second or Third World, reach radically different policy prescriptions for the current recession and divergent evaluations of the monetarist approach. The monetarist position is represented by Mundell and Polak.[1] Mundell, as a 'global' monetarist, argues that inflation and the recession can best be combated by the restoration of stability and discipline in the international monetary system through a return to fixed exchange rates. Polak, also a monetarist but less optimistic about the possibilities of international monetary reform, stresses the need for national monetary policy to check inflation and thus restore confidence and productive investment. Heertje agrees with Polak on this matter, although he does not share the more ideological commitment of some monetarists to the superior efficiency of the market mechanism.

Cripps, Seers, Van Arkadie and Jayawardena, each in his own way, maintain the post-Keynesian or Structuralist position that the free market mechanism may result in unstable or otherwise undesirable outcomes and that, therefore, state intervention is necessary to steer and stabilise economic development.

Ellman makes the interesting point that whereas in supply-constrained economies (in his case the state socialist economies, but many developing countries also fit that category) monetarist policies to control inflation may be both feasible and progres-

3

sive, in demand-constrained economies this is typically not the case. Seers and Van Arkadie seem to agree with this position in that they both stress the need for cautious monetary and fiscal policies in developing countries in the process of economic restructuring.

Finally, Mandel, as representative of the Marxist tradition, considers the current crisis to be one in the series of inevitable crises of capitalism. He considers monetarism as a policy and an ideology which has to cover attempts to restore profits.

The remainder of this introductory chapter serves two purposes. First, the main contours of the current recession will be analysed, thus setting the stage on which economic policy is at present conducted. The main purpose, however, is to describe and analyse monetarist policy as conducted in different parts of the world, as well as the criticisms that have been brought against it. This will be done in the third section, which will draw heavily on the other contributions to the book.

THE CONTOURS OF THE CRISIS

The term 'economic crisis' has ominous overtones, bringing to mind *the* economic crisis, the Great Depression of the 1930s. Comments on the current crisis regularly make this linkage to its historical precedent, and it may therefore be useful to recall the main characteristics of the Great Depression. In the years after 1929 real output fell profoundly and world trade collapsed in both volume and value terms. The result was enormous unemployment, leading to a reduction in nominal wages; as prices also fell, however, real wages remained constant or even increased. Profits were slashed and there was a virtual investment stop. Money stocks fell, as did short-term rates of interest.[2] The financial system, national and international, experienced a major crisis. In the USA many banks had to close, and in Europe bank failures and threats of failure led to currency crises which forced governments to intervene or to leave the gold standard, as Britain did in 1931.

As the following description of the current crisis will show, however, history has not repeated itself.

Production and Trade

Tables 1 and 2 on growth trends and patterns in production and in world trade give a first indication of the economic problems of the 1970s. There is a significant deceleration in the rate of economic growth of industrial countries as well as of those developing countries whose economic fate is more intimately linked with the developed world.[3] Trends in export volumes show a similar trend. The low-income developing countries had little share in the pre-1973 growth boom, and after 1973 their growth rates remained at levels that only just allowed an increase in per capita income. The growth rates of the centrally planned economies which are not represented in Table 1, remained at relatively high levels throughout the 1970s.[4]

TABLE 1

Production: Average Annual Rate of Growth★

	1962-72	1973-79	1980-82
Industrial countries	4.8	3.3	1.1
	1967-72		
Developing countries:			
oil exporting countries	9.0	5.9	−2.8
non-oil developing countries:			
net oil exporters	6.0	6.3	6.3
net oil importers:			
– major exporters of manufactures	8.1	6.0	2.6
– low income countries ★★	3.4	3.6	4.0
– other	5.5	4.7	3.3

★For industrial countries real GNP and for developing countries real GDP.
★★Excluding People's Republic of China.
Source: IMF [*1981a; 1982*]. For a comment on the country grouping see note 3.

TABLE 2

Volume of World Trade and Purchasing Power of Exports: Average Annual Rates of Growth

	Volume of Trade			Purchasing Power of Exports**		
	1963-72	1973-79	1980-82	1968-72	1973-79	1980-82
World Trade	8.5	5.9	1.3	—	—	—
Exports:						
Industrial Countries	9.0	6.3	3.1	9.3***	4.1	0.7
Developing countries:						
Oil exporting countries	9.1	2.3	-12.7	9.6***	18.0	2.2
Non-oil developing countries:						
– net oil exporters	6.7	6.2	5.3	8.4	6.3	2.7
– net oil importers:	5.3*	4.7	5.4	3.8	11.2	5.7
– major exporters of manufactures	11.8*	9.1	5.6	12.6	8.0	4.0
– low income countries	5.5*	3.2	2.2	6.1	0.9	-6.6
– other	6.7*	2.9	4.3	5.2	2.7	-2.5

*1968-72.
**Export earnings deflated by import prices. (Data on Purchasing Power of Exports for industrial countries and for oil-exporting developing countries have been calculated by the author using data from IMF [1982].)
***1963-72 average.
Source: IMF [1982].

The decline in the rate of growth of the volume of world trade shown in Table 2 is a direct result of the fall in the rate of growth in real output. The trends in the purchasing power of exports also reflect differential trends in the world market prices for oil, industrial products and primary commodities. Developing countries which export primary commodities and which, according to Table 1, have more or less maintained their modest growth rates of production, experienced a very sharp fall in the growth of the volume of their exports and complete stagnation or even decline in the purchasing power of those exports. In contrast, the more diversified developing countries, i.e. those non-oil developing countries with significant exports of manufactured goods, had high rates of growth in their export volume and the purchasing power of their exports continued to increase.

The data in Tables 1 and 2 lead to two additional observations. First, both tables show that the recession deepened towards the end of the 1970s and in the early 1980s, suggesting that the current recession is deeper than others in the post-war period. There is even reason to suggest, as Mandel does, that we have entered a depression in the long waves of capitalist development.

The second observation is that the growth patterns displayed in Tables 1 and 2 are indicative of separate developments in the various parts of what was *the* Third World. In the 1960s and 1970s a number of non-oil developing countries successfully diversified their production and export structures away from the primary commodity bias (in our tables these countries are found in the groups 'major exporters of manufactures' and 'net oil exporters'; elsewhere such countries are often referred to as newly industrialised countries, NICs). These countries showed high rates of growth of output and exports during the 1960s and also did relatively well during the difficult years of the 1970s, although some were only able to maintain that performance by accumulating very large external debts. The emergence of this group of countries is indicative of the changing international division of labour and, as such, is one of the factors responsible for the unemployment problem in the industrial countries.

7

Karel Jansen

Unemployment and Inflation

Although production has not fallen to the same degree as in the Great Depression, unemployment in the industrial countries has increased rapidly, becoming the principal common factor of the crisis of the 1930s and of today, and the main reason for the analogy drawn between the two crises. In the industrial countries taken together, employment continued to grow over the entire period 1963-81, although in most European countries there was a stagnation in the growth of employment or even a slight decline in the 1970s.[5] The growth of employment was so slow, however, that it led to a rapid increase in unemployment and in the rate of unemployment. The fact that in the 1960s, when economic growth was still rapid in the industrial countries, the growth of employment was modest and unemployment started to increase, suggests that the cause of the rising unemployment should not be sought exclusively in the slowdown of economic growth. Various other more structural factors have contributed to the stagnation in employment, such as technological progress resulting in labour saving, an international division of labour that shifts labour-intensive production to cheap-labour countries, and inefficiencies and rigidities in the labour market of industrial countries which prevent rapid adjustment and extend unemployment.

In the 1960s, in industrial countries, the growth of labour productivity started to slow down;[6] if that had not been the case, unemployment might still have been higher. As it was not accompanied by a decline in the growth of nominal wages, unit labour cost increased and inflation was stimulated.

This wage push factor was only one of the reasons for the acceleration of inflation in the industrial countries shown in Table 3. That acceleration had started even in the 1960s, and the oil price increase of 1973 added fuel to what was already a brisk fire. In the last year or so there has been a decline in the rate of inflation in the USA, as Polak observes in his contribution, and more generally in the industrial countries,[7] which some have ascribed to the success of monetarist policies. Both before and since 1973 inflation has been higher in developing countries than in the industrial world. One explanation of this is

8

TABLE 3

Consumer Prices: Average Annual Rate of Increase

	1967-72	1973-79	1980-82
Industrial countries*	4.2***	8.7	8.3
Developing countries:			
Oil exporting countries	8.0	14.3	11.6
Non-oil developing countries:			
net oil exporters	4.1	17.0	28.5
net oil importers:			
– major exporters of manufactures	14.1	37.8	55.8
– low income countries**	6.6	13.3	16.0
– other	8.6	26.5	24.4

*OECD countries.
**Excluding People's Republic of China.
***1963-72.
Source: as Table 1.

given by the structuralist interpretation of inflation, summarised by Seers, which argues that the growth and restructuring of developing countries runs into supply rigidities and other bottlenecks which lead to inflation.

It is remarkable that those non-oil developing countries with the most diversified economic structures which were best able to adjust to the external shocks of the 1970s, i.e. the NICs, have also suffered the highest rates of inflation.

The combination of elements described so far – slow growth together with unemployment and inflation – has caused adoption of the term 'stagflation' to characterise the current crisis. The fact that the end of the period of high and stable growth rates more or less coincided with the oil price increase of 1973 initially led commentators to see the oil price hike as *the* exogeneous factor which triggered off the recession. Important elements of the recession in the industrial countries, however, such as the decline in labour productivity growth, the acceleration of inflation, the increase in the rate of unemployment and the breakdown of the Bretton Woods system of fixed exchange rates, occurred well before 1973. In many respects the oil price increase can be interpreted as a reaction to those events rather than as an exogeneous factor. To turn the oil price increase into an endogeneous shock, of course, does not lessen its effect. On the contrary, industrial countries which were already facing economic difficulties before the oil price hike, have been more vulnerable and less able to deal with the ensuing crisis.

For the non-oil developing countries the 1973 increase was both an external and an exogeneous shock. The second oil price shock of 1979 may have come less as a surprise than the first, but a number of developing countries which had just managed to make their adjustments to the first increase were hard hit.

A fundamental problem with the two oil price shocks, as Cripps points out, is that when a crucial market such as the oil market runs in such unstable patterns, there is little hope for overall economic stability. Jayawardena also addresses this problem, claiming that durable solutions to the economic problems of poor countries require some form of stabilisation of the oil market, and discussing some proposals that have been made to that end.

The present instability of the oil market and of the entire world economy have found expression in sharply increased current account imbalances.

Current Account Deficits

Table 4 shows current account deficits as percentages of GDP for the various categories of oil-importing countries. The fluctuations in the current accounts of the industrial countries appear to be much less severe than those of the developing countries. This conclusion also holds if we look at the absolute size of deficits rather than at proportions of GDP. The reasons for this are that industrial countries were able to increase their exports to the oil countries and also to increase the prices of their industrial exports in order to compensate for the import price jump. After 1973, moreover, and again after the 1979 oil price increase, the industrial countries entered a sharp recession which reduced their import demand.

TABLE 4

Current Account Deficits* as Percentage of GDP of Oil-Importing Countries

	1970	1971	1972	1973	1974	1975	1976	1977	1978	1979	1980	1981
Industrial Countries**	(0.3)	(0.5)	(0.4)	(0.3)	0.7	(0.1)	0.4	0.4	(0.2)	0.5	0.8	—
Non-oil Developing Countries:												
net oil exporters	—	—	—	2.0	5.0	5.8	3.7	3.0	3.2	4.0	4.8	4.9
net oil importers:	—	—	—	2.9	4.5	7.3	5.3	4.4	4.3	3.8	3.8	4.3
– major exporters of manufactures	—	—	—	1.5	6.2	6.0	3.2	1.9	2.0	3.5	4.3	4.4
– low income countries	—	—	—	3.1	4.9	4.7	2.6	1.8	3.1	4.0	4.7	4.4
– other	—	—	—	0.9	3.1	5.3	4.3	4.8	4.8	5.0	6.5	6.7

*A surplus is indicated by brackets ().
**OECD countries.
Source: For OECD countries, OECD *Economic Outlook* [*December 1981*] and for other countries IMF [*1981a*].

11

The reaction of the developing countries was quite different. They were unable to increase their exports to the oil countries to any significant extent (although for a few the remittances by labour exported to the Gulf states became a major source of foreign exchange earnings), nor could the prices of their primary commodities exports be raised. Probably because the oil price increase was to them a more sudden and exogeneous shock, they found it difficult to adjust rapidly. Thus, many of them maintained their import levels in the face of declining export earnings by increasing external borrowing. As a result, the long-term external debt of non-oil developing countries increased rapidly from US$ 97 billion in 1973 to 505 billion in 1982 [*IMF, 1982: 70*]. Short-term debt also increased significantly.

An IMF study into the external indebtedness of developing countries [*1981: 5, 9*] has observed that growth in the debt, when measured in real terms, was *lower* in the 1970s than it had been in the 1960s. Debt servicing, again in real terms, had increased at about the same rate in the two decades; in other words, in the 1970s more of the debt was from private creditors at higher cost, while interest rates were higher.

The same source also indicates the extreme concentration of the external debt. Of the recorded medium and long-term debt in 1979, five countries (Brazil, Mexico, Algeria, India and Indonesia) accounted for 35 per cent of total debt and the biggest ten debtors for 51 per cent. As a result, the debt servicing ratio (debt servicing as percentage of exports of goods and services) of the non-oil developing countries increased from seven per cent in 1960 to 16 per cent in 1970, dropped to 14 per cent in 1975 and rose again to 19 per cent in 1979.[8] These data on the debt burden are averages which conceal significant variations among countries. For some the debt burden became excessive, forcing them to enter into multilateral debt renegotiations when they failed to meet their debt servicing obligations.[9]

Data on the external debt position of the centrally-planned economies are more difficult to obtain, but it is known that Poland and Romania, for example, have substantial external debts. For them, as for the developing countries with significant external debts, the high interest rate on the

TABLE 5

Long-term External Debt and Debt Servicing Ratio
of Non-Oil Developing Countries

	1973	1975	1980	1982
	Total outstanding debt (billion US$)			
Total non-oil developing countries	96.8	146.8	375.4	505.2
Net oil exporters	15.6	31.0	78.0	107.0
Net oil importers:	81.2	115.8	297.4	398.2
– major exporters of manufactures	38.3	55.8	143.4	194.1
– low income countries	21.6	29.1	62.3	79.7
– other	21.3	30.9	91.7	124.3
	Debt servicing ratio (percentages)★			
Total non-oil developing countries	14.0	14.0	16.3	22.3
Net oil exporters	20.9	19.3	24.4	37.1
Net oil importers:				
– major exporters of manufactures	14.8	14.9	15.4	20.1
– low income countries	12.6	13.0	10.5	14.1
– other	10.0	10.1	15.8	21.4

★Debt payments (interest plus amortisation) as percentage of exports of goods and services.
Source: IMF [*1982: 170, 173*].

international capital market – which finds its origin in the industrial countries – is a principal element of the economic crisis that they are experiencing.

Table 5 shows that the privatisation of capital flows to the developing countries has resulted in their increasing concentration on the better-off countries. The low-income countries which, given their low growth rates (see Table 1), and the disastrous development of their export earnings (see Table 2), stand most in need of capital inflow, had the lowest growth of external debt over the 1970s, although the amounts involved were still large enough to finance sizeable current account deficits. It is not surprising, of course, that the richer and more diversified developing countries have preferential access to international credit, but in the 1970s this had the consequence that the international private capital market became an important instrument in shaping a new international division of labour. Another effect of the increased international capital flows to developing countries has been that the inflow of that capital has often had an expansionary effect on their total liquidity, and thus has been partly responsible for the acceleration of inflation in these countries (see Table 3).

After the oil price hikes of 1973 and 1979, the industrial countries increased their export prices and entered a recession, which enabled them to reduce their current account deficits. The non-oil developing countries were thus hit twice: first by the oil price increase and the subsequent inflation in industrial prices, and then by the decline in the industrial countries' demand for their exports. In the face of adversity, the developing countries were able to maintain their import levels to some extent by increasing their indebtedness in order to finance current account deficits. The willingness of developing countries to follow this expansionary path and the ability of the financial system to finance it has alleviated the impact of the economic crisis. In recent years, the current account deficit of the combined non-oil developing countries has been equivalent to between five and seven per cent of the exports of the industrial countries. It might be suggested that this process is a form of international Keynesianism whereby the unspent savings of one part of the world economy – OPEC – are transformed into spending by another part. *Ex post*, of course, the deficit of one country or of a group of countries has to be balanced by another's surplus; *strictu sensu*, moreover, it cannot be said that the deficit causes or enables a surplus elsewhere, or vice versa. But in fact, policy makers are more concerned about current account deficits than about surpluses, and it could thus be asserted that the willingness and ability to run the former determines the latter.

The internationalisation of financial markets and the

increased mobility of capital has made this process possible. But it has not been without its problems. As Jayawardena indicates, external borrowing has concentrated on a small number of developing countries, some of which are now reaching the limits of their debt carrying capacity. The poor developing countries, in particular, are omitted from the process. Proposals to guarantee a more extended process of international Keynesianism are reviewed in Jayawardena's contribution.

The Nature of the Crisis

The description given so far of the contours of the crisis is perhaps rather aggregative. Each country has to face its own crisis, of course, and the particular manifestations and intensity of that crisis are determined by external factors as well as by national characteristics. There are enough common elements and world-wide trends, however, to justify some more general conclusions.

In the industrial countries the crisis is felt to be one of the domestic economy, reflected in such phenomena as inflation, slow growth and unemployment, and captured by the term 'stagflation'. For the non-oil developing countries it is clearly a crisis of the external sector with increasing oil and other import prices, low prices and a weak demand for most primary export commodities. And to this could be added the high rates of interest on the external debt in recent years.

There can be no doubt that the poor, primary commodity-exporting developing countries in particular, have suffered deeply from the crisis. The story of Tanzania, given in Van Arkadie's contribution, is to some extent typical of other sub-Saharan African countries. An external crisis, of course, will inevitably bring out any weaknesses in the domestic economy and in the development strategy of a country, and it is easy for outsiders, in their analyses and policy advice, to concentrate on those internal weaknesses rather than on the external origins of the economic crisis that is hitting the country. The principal factor to determine the fate of a developing country in the economic crisis of the 1970s seems to have been the position that the country had in the world economy at the start of the crisis. Those developing countries which had more diversified economic structures and export bases have been better able to deal with the crisis than the primary commodities-exporting countries. Unfortunately, of course, the latter category contains the majority of developing countries.

The economic literature does not suffer from any dearth of interpretations of the crisis. We shall deal selectively with some of the approaches in this introductory chapter, concentrating in particular on the views presented by the contributors to this book.

According to most interpretations, the recession originated in the industrial countries where the stagnation in economic growth and the increase in unemployment is attributed to the decline in private investment.[10] This investment fall is due to longer-term processes such as the erosion of corporate profitability, the uncertainty created by inflation and variable rates of exchange, and the growing burden of taxes on income which reduce the incentive to work and to invest. These longer-term processes have been reinforced and deepened by the oil price increases and, more recently, by the high rates of interest.[11] Within this general description of the causes of the recession, to which most economists seem to subscribe, individual authors place their own emphasis.

Mundell argues that the end of the dollar's convertibility into gold and of the fixed exchange rates for major currencies meant the end of an international system which had imposed discipline on national monetary authorities and governments. Flexible exchange rates caused each country to become responsible for its own inflation rate, and the lack of any externally imposed discipline resulted in an acceleration of inflation which in turn undermined expectations, investment and growth. Acceleration in the rates of inflation in industrial countries started as long ago as the 1960s, so that it could be argued that discipline had softened even before the collapse of the Bretton Woods system. Indeed, some have argued that the differential rates of inflation between the major economies was the main reason for the breakdown of Bretton Woods' fixed exchange rates. It is a fact, however, that after 1969 a very rapid acceleration occurred in the growth of international liquidities.[12]

Cripps sees the instability of the international economic system as caused by the unequal geographical distribution of growth rates of production and of trade. Relatively successful industrial countries see their production and exports grow rapidly, relatively unsuccessful countries see them grow only slowly. As a result, industrial production becomes concentrated in a few countries, while unsuccessful countries acquire current account deficits. To the extent that these countries are unwilling or unable to finance their deficits by increasing their external debt, they are forced into deflation in order to close the current account.[13] Thus, production in the industrial countries as a totality will fall below its full employment potential, while developing countries are also affected because demand for their primary commodities is less than it could be. The monetary instability emphasised by Mundell seems to Cripps to reflect the underlying imbalances in the real economy.[14]

Mandel, in the Marxist tradition, sees in the present recession one of the recurrent crises of the capitalist system. He emphasises the dual nature of the crisis: there is over-production of capital and of commodities, i.e. a simultaneous occurrence of a fall in profitability and lack of purchasing power. The fall in profitability started in the 1960s,[15] and is ascribed by Mandel to the over-accumulation of capital and the resulting under-consumption of commodities.

Other authors have suggested different causes of the fall in profit shares. Some have argued that the full employment policies of governments of industrial countries have strengthened the hand of the trade unions, leading to rapid increases in real wages and in the wage share which were not redressed in the 1970s when the growth of labour productivity decelerated (see, for example, Rowthorn [1977]).

Another attack on the profit share is made by the public sector's increasing claim on available income. In the OECD countries the share of Final Government Consumption Expenditure in GDP rose from 15 per cent in 1960, to 16.3 per cent in 1970, to 17.1 per cent in 1980; Current Receipts of Government as percentage of GDP increased from 28.3 per cent

17

in 1960, to 31.9 per cent in 1970, and 34.8 per cent in 1978.[16] Given the above comments on the wage share, it is quite likely that in most industrial countries this increasing claim of the public sector has been at the expense of the profit share.

While in industrial countries profits and profit expectations are central to the explanation of private investment behaviour and thus of fluctuations in economic growth, for developing countries the situation is more complex. Statistical data on the profit rate and profit share in developing countries are scarce, but that which is available suggests an experience quite different to that of the industrial countries. It is clear that in quite a number of developing countries real wages, and probably also the wage share, fell sharply in the 1970s.[17] Claims by the public sector increased as in the industrial countries, but there were also significant terms-of-trade losses. The overall effect of these trends on profits is not clear. In the developing countries, however, good profits are not sufficient to guarantee investments: without their own investment goods sector, the transformation of profits and of public sector savings into investments requires the import of investment goods, and thus the availability of foreign exchange. Stagnation in the purchasing power of their exports may thus be a more important constraint on investment than past or expected profits. The relative stability of growth rates (see Table 1) of some non-oil developing countries suggests that they have maintained their levels of investment despite the stagnation in export earnings. This might be explained by two factors. First, consumption levels and the imports of consumption goods were significantly reduced together with the reduction in real wages observed above. Second, the inflow of international credit allowed them to maintain their investments. International loans, particularly long-term ones, tend to be linked to specific investment projects. Thus, the increase in external debt can in itself lead to a relative increase in the investment share in total expenditure. For some of these countries it might be questioned, as Van Arkadie does for Tanzania, whether investment levels are not maintained at too high a level, thus reducing the foreign exchange available for the operation and maintenance of existing plants and for essential consumption imports. The fact that external finance is readily available for investment projects may mean that current account deficits, in themselves, shift resources from consumption to investment. On the other hand, in some countries the availability of external loans has been used to maintain consumption levels and imports which had become unrealistic in the face of declining export earnings and increased import prices.[18]

Monetarists see inflation as the main manifestation and principal cause of the economic crisis. Whatever 'real' factors are said to be behind inflation, it is the expansion of the money supply which ultimately allows these factors and pressures to be reflected in general price increases rather than in relative price adjustments that would clear the troubled markets.

Inflation, as Polak indicates, affects expectations and increases uncertainties, and in this way has a negative influence on investment and economic growth.[19] Global monetarists such as Mundell, seek the principal source of inflation in the instability of the international monetary system and the excessive growth in international liquidities, whereas monetarists like Polak primarily hold individual countries responsible for their own rate of inflation. Both agree in their judgment of the adverse effects of inflation, but differ significantly in their policy prescriptions, as we shall see later.

After this discussion on the contours of the economic crisis, we have to conclude that that which is experienced by industrial countries as a crisis of the domestic economy, reflected in such phenomena as inflation and unemployment, is for the developing countries a crisis of the balance of payments, of export earnings and external debt.

This difference in experience and perception is significant for any understanding of the directions in which solutions have been sought. The economic crisis has led both industrial and developing countries to an evaluation of conventional economic policy and to a search for new approaches which are likely to be more successful in dealing with the crisis. The trend in economic policy thinking now seems to be away from Keynesianism and development planning, and towards monetarism and the market mechanism. The reasons for this shift, the policies it leads to, and the effects of those policies are the subject of the next section.

Karel Jansen

MONETARISM AS AN ECONOMIC POLICY

The current economic crisis has brought with it a noted shift in economic policy, in theory, in public debate and, to a considerable extent, also in practice. Conventional Keynesian economic thinking would let the state intervene in the recession through expansionary fiscal policy. But not in the 1970s: in all parts of the world – in industrial and in developing countries, and also in some centrally-planned economies such as Hungary and the People's Republic of China – there has been a move against activist state intervention and regulation and towards greater market autonomy. Keynesian economics in the industrial countries and development planning in the Third World were the guiding principles for economic policy in the 1950s and 1960s. They are based on the belief that the state is more rational than the private sector and can thus correct any market imbalances that the private sector may create, and can contribute, mainly through fiscal policy, to achieving the important and overriding policy objective: full employment. Development planning is based on the assumption that the state has to take the initiative and leadership in the process of economic growth and restructuring. These beliefs and assumptions have always been under attack, but only in the 1970s did that attack become influential. Why? We believe that Keynesian economic policy and development planning went into decline because (a) priorities with respect to policy objectives changed and the effectiveness of certain policy instruments was reduced, and (b) the international context in which national economic policy making takes place underwent drastic change. The first set of factors can be summarised as follows.

First, full employment is only one of the objectives of economic policy and can be maintained as predominant only as long as the other objectives (inflation, balance of payments equilibrium, economic growth, etc.) remain at acceptable levels. The acceleration of inflation destroyed that equilibrium. While some would claim that policies of continuous full employment were responsible for the acceleration of inflation – through some kind of Phillips-curve effect – and others would argue that inflation was due to other causes, the increasing level of the rate

20

of inflation made it a policy problem. And in the eyes of Polak and other monetarists, into a policy problem of the first order.[20] Keynesian economists suggested incomes policies and price controls as instruments with which to control inflation, but this approach has been denounced by the monetarists as ineffective and undesirable.

Moreover, to the extent that unemployment is due to more structural and institutional factors, as I have suggested above that it might well be, Keynesian macro-economic policies will be unable to solve this problem, although Cripps would argue that even under such conditions an expansionary policy will be best able to combat both inflation and unemployment.[21]

Second, Keynesian economic policy is associated with active state intervention and, rightly or wrongly, with an expanding public sector. Even if it is argued that the increase in the relative size of the public sector should be attributed to other factors,[22] it could still be maintained that resistance to that expansion has been lessened by the Keynesian possibility of an unbalanced budget. In the 1970s, concern about the growing size of the public sector and about the increasing budget deficits, found expression in the debate about 'crowding out', suggesting a conflict between the growth of the private sector and expansion of the public sector. In developing countries, concern about the excessive size of the state is expressed in complaints about inefficient bureaucracies and corruption, and about the excessive state regulation of trade and investment. The crisis of the 1970s contributed to this problem. In industrial countries state revenue fell with income, whereas expenditure increased with social security payments for the unemployed and hikes in military spending. The resulting growth in the budget deficit became a matter of intense concern, preventing a more active Keynesian policy which threatened to increase that deficit even further. In the developing countries, the same effects on government revenue and expenditure could be observed to some extent, and similar concern about the budget deficit and its inflationary impact was expressed.

Third, Keynesian policies became ineffective in the crisis of the 1970s. The assumption of an expansionary fiscal policy is that it will lead, through multiplier and accelerator effects, to an expansion of investment. But as Mandel points out, the

21

investment decision has two aspects: expectations of sales and of profits. The long-term decline in profits that I observed (page 17 and note 15) made fiscal stimulation of sales insufficient. The governments of developing countries would meet with similar problems if they were to try to stimulate private investment, not so much due to the lack of profits as to the lack of foreign exchange caused by the crisis.

In the industrial countries, therefore, concern about inflation and about the expanding state sector and increased budget deficits, together with the fall in profits, made Keynesian policies both unwanted and ineffective. This move against active state intervention in the economy is also to be observed in the developing countries, partly due to the fact that economics is a Western-oriented science in which the major policy orientations of the dominant economies are reflected in the policy advice which is given to developing countries. More objective factors have also played a role, but these can better be discussed after we have considered the second set of factors which led to the shift in economic policy perspectives: changes in the international context.

It is not remarkably original to observe that national economies have become more and more internationalised and integrated into the world economy, but the implications for economic policy making are not always drawn sufficiently. The internationalisation has occurred on both product and factor markets. The internationalisation of production can best be seen by comparing Table 1 and Table 2. This will show that growth rates of the volume of exports have been in excess of those of real GDP in both the industrial countries and the developing world. The recession of the 1970s changed that relationship for the oil-exporting countries – although they had compensating terms-of-trade gains – and for some of the primary commodities exporters. Export production came to represent an increased share of total production, about 20 per cent on average in industrial and in non-oil developing countries, while imports made up a larger share of demand. This implies that a Keynesian policy of stimulating domestic demand sooner runs into balance of payments problems. It also means that export'growth became a main avenue to economic recovery: in the industrial countries because low population growth and the need to keep real wages down in order to restore profits reduced domestic demand, and in the Third World because the growth of exports determines the import capacity, which in turn is a major determinant of investment and growth.

The internationalisation of production has largely been effected through multinational corporations, the emergence of which creates an economic group whose production, pricing and investment decisions are influenced by economic conditions and policies in several countries – a fact which reduces the effectiveness of any individual country's economic policy.

The internationalisation of factor markets has been most dramatic in the money and capital markets. The estimated size of the Eurocurrency market has increased from US$12 billion in 1964, to 75 billion in 1970, to 259 billion in 1975, and 840 billion in 1981 [*BIS, 1982*]. This rapid growth is related to the expansion of world trade and of the multinational corporations, but the increased international mobility of capital which it implies has had other important consequences. First of these, is that it has enabled the financing of the large current account deficits of some non-oil developing countries and of some East European countries. A second implication of the internationalisation of the capital market, more important in the present context, is that it has significantly reduced the autonomy of national policy making. For instance, high interest rates on the international market have made it impossible to uphold Keynesian-inspired policies aimed at depressing interest rates in order to stimulate investment, while low interest rates would have led to an outflow of capital rather than to investment, or to large and undesired fluctuations in the exchange rate.

All these aspects of the internationalisation process seem to have reduced the autonomy and effectiveness of national policy making. Keynesian demand-stimulating policies come sooner into contact with balance of payments constraints. Exports, which have become the major dynamic component of final demand, are in fact beyond the control of Keynesian policies. Moreover, demand expansion may not lead to an acceleration process as the multinational corporations have made investment reactions more uncertain; and low interest rates may lead to capital outflow rather than investment.

23

Karel Jansen

Monetarists have claimed that flexible exchange rates would make each country responsible for its own inflation rate and would thus restore national policy autonomy. This is of little relevance to developing countries with their pegged exchange rates, but practice has been different even for industrial countries. The international mobility of capital has maintained a much higher degree of interdependence between countries than the theory of flexible exchange rates would have led one to expect.

In summary, monetarism came to the forefront of the economic policy scene when priorities shifted to the fight against inflation, to reduction of the size of, and intervention by, the state, and to the restoration of profitability through wage reduction; and when the international context became more of a constraint on national policy-making autonomy, for developing countries in particular, through a tightening of the balance of payments constraint, and through reduced national control over trade, investment and capital flows. Any evaluation of monetarism must assess to what extent, in theory and in practice, it meets those conditions.

Monetarism and Inflation

Monetarists are proud to stress that they belong to a long and respectable tradition in economic science: the Quantity Theory of Money. That lineage, together with its modern reformulation by Milton Friedman, provides a ready explanation and remedy for inflation. The key positive tenet of practical monetarism is, in Laidler's words, that 'monetary weapons should be assigned to the attainment and maintenance of long-run price stability' [*Laidler, 1981: 21*]. But the choice as to which monetary weapon should be assigned to that task has caused a sharp divide between various groups of monetarists. To quote Laidler again, 'A fixed exchange rate is one way of tying down monetary policy, and the adoption of some sort of a money supply growth rule would be an alternative' [*Ibidem: 20*]. A necessary prerequisite of this alternative is a flexible exchange rate, and this is the particular combination which a number of industrial countries have tried. In Laidler's opinion, this has not been done with any great success, although more

24

recent data show a decline in the rate of inflation of many industrial countries.[23] The decline is slow, however, and inflation remains at high levels.

In his evaluation of monetarist policies in Latin America, Seers concludes that they have not always been successful in reducing the rate of inflation, and that, where inflation has indeed been brought down, it has often been at the expense of an overvalued exchange rate, increased external debt and high social costs, making it doubtful whether the success could be sustained. The Latin American countries had fixed exchange rates in principle of course, but devaluations were so common that the distinction with flexible rates seemed to disappear.

Many have argued, on theoretical[24] and on practical grounds against the possibility of control over money supply. Mundell states that the proper definition of the monetary aggregate to be controlled is problematic, and its actual control in an economy with open links to the international capital market impossible. He further emphasises that, in the absence of gold convertibility and fixed exchange rates, the monetary authorities will lack the discipline necessary for control of the money supply. In this respect it is interesting to refer to Ellman who mentions that monetarist thought regarding inflation control fits well with the ideas and institutional realities of what he calls the State Socialist Economies, where the real economy is determined by real factors (planning) and inflation is considered harmful. Given the desired price level in the economy, the quantity of money is set and institutions are capable of controlling it. In Ellman's judgment, monetarist-like anti-inflation policies are both feasible and progressive in State Socialist Economies, which are supply-constrained and never demand-constrained.

Polak and Heertje maintain that some workable definition of the money supply can also be found in capitalist economies, that it could be controlled by a sufficiently strong and independent monetary authority, and that inflation could thus be brought under control. They realise that this may be preceded by a period of hardship in the form of unemployment and slow growth, but claim that the hardship of a permanent world stagflation, which is the only alternative, would in the end be greater.

In conclusion, it seems that monetarists share a priority aim:

the fight against inflation in order to restore stability and confidence which will lead to a recovery of investments – but differ sharply as to what would be the best policy instrument to bring this about. The 'quantity rule' line has predominated in policy application but does not yet show a convincing track record; where success has been achieved it has been at high cost, which is admitted but claimed to be necessary.

Monetarism and the Economic Role of the State

According to Cripps, a basic characteristic of monetarism is its neo-classical belief in the market mechanism: markets are cleared through (relative) price movements. Some monetarists would admit that price adjustments may be slow in some markets and that, in the short run, quantity adjustments may dominate and create shocks; nevertheless, they will maintain that prices will settle at market-clearing levels in the long run. They would also deny that fine-tuning policies introduced by the government might be capable of correcting these short-term shocks: given information and reaction lags, policies are likely to be pro-cyclical rather than anti-cyclical.[25] Although the opposition to fine-tuning in itself says nothing about a preference for a particular size of the public sector or a particular degree of state intervention, it would be reasonable to say that monetarists in general prefer a smaller rather than a larger public sector, and less rather than more state intervention.

Cripps and Heertje criticise the monetarist position on the relative role of the market and the state, observing that the real world is composed of monopolistic firms which adjust the quantities they supply to demand fluctuations rather than their prices. The outcome of such behaviour is unstable markets which can easily settle at less than full capacity equilibria. Cripps posits that not only national markets but also international markets are unstable, and that the national and supra-national regulation of such markets is inevitable and necessary. The futility of economic science is illustrated by the fact that, after the failure of deflationary policies in the 1930s, the insight of Kalecki and Keynes that (monopolistic) industrial economies do not automatically tend towards full employment equilibrium, was narrowed down in the neo-classical synthesis to an argument about aggregate demand, was then rediscovered by Leijonhufvud, only to be lost again in the present upsurge of neo-classical economics. A possible explanation of these shifts may be derived from Heertje's interpretation, i.e. that where, in the industrial economies, fiscal policies and price and income policies have failed to bring inflation under control and, given the nature of the political process, could not be expected to do so, a strict monetary policy executed by a strong and independent central bank may be necessary to create a situation in which appropriate adjustments in the real sector will be made. This would suggest that the case for the market mechanism and against too much active state intervention might be based on a practical judgment of the political process and of the effects of macro-economic policy rather than on any underlying belief as to how markets really work. But then the question also becomes whether monetarism better fits with the reality of the political process and whether, in practice, it is able to achieve its policy objectives.

The Latin American debate between structuralists and monetarists, summarised by Seers, can in many respects also be interpreted as a debate about the role of the state. The structuralists see the developing countries as having one-sided economic structures facing unstable export markets, technologically dependent, with a small corporate sector which is dominated by a few large monopolistic firms; above all, as countries with numerous institutional obstacles and bottlenecks. All these elements are characteristic of an economy with low elasticities of supply and limited substitution possibilities, where price signals are unlikely to be effective. The need then arises for state intervention, which is not always or necessarily against the private sector; public sector activities and state intervention may well be necessary to make private sector investment at all possible. An unfortunate consequence is that the resulting rapid rise in government expenditure is insufficiently balanced by an increase in revenue and has to be paid for by money creation, leading to further inflation.

The monetarist position in that debate, on both theoretical and practical grounds, is that market solutions are superior. State intervention will lead to distorted prices, inefficiency and, in the end, a lower growth of production and welfare. In the

Latin American debate, this monetarist position was articulated largely by IMF representatives. Even today, the policies demanded from those countries that seek standby agreements with the IMF are inspired by these ideas.

Van Arkadie's account of the Tanzanian experience – which is similar to that of quite a number of other countries – shows that the IMF is concerned about distorted prices such as rates of exchange, rates of interest, import tariffs, state enterprise prices and real wages, and about the rapid growth of public expenditure. The use of the term 'distorted prices' provides an easy opening for the criticism that in an economic reality of monopolistic firms, high tax burdens and institutional rigidities, all prices are distorted, and that market solutions also suffer from the shortcoming. This is the Keynesian position: private sector prices are distorted and lead to disequilibria which have to be corrected by government intervention. Such criticism is not sufficient, however; even if all prices are distorted, there can be a practical debate about which prices should be most distorted and in what direction. The IMF position can then be interpreted thus: the rate of exchange, import tariffs, tax rates, and real wages are too high, and interest rates and state enterprise prices too low.

Governments of developing countries distort prices purposefully in order to obtain a resource allocation between consumption and investment and between various sectors of the economy which will be better than one obtained with 'undistorted prices'. Rather than to condemn price distortions on theoretical grounds, it is appropriate to ask whether the distortions and controls have been successful in achieving government objectives, and if so, whether under the changing internal and international conditions the same distortions and controls should be maintained, or whether changes in policy objectives and instruments are called for. Van Arkadie deals with these matters in his analysis of the situation in Tanzania, and below we shall deal with them in a more general context.

Monetarism and Profits and Investment

Polak argues that inflation results in uncertainties which will tend to decrease investments, and will shift them towards

28

financial investments and speculation or to projects with low productivity but stable value, and away from productive investment. These are the real costs of inflation, the successful combating of which can be expected to lead to more productive investment.

I have commented earlier about the decline in profit rates and shares in industrial countries and doubt whether in itself the control of inflation will be sufficient to restore investment. Mandel interprets the shift to monetarism as a shift in the priorities of the ruling class towards the creation of conditions for the restoration of profitability: priorities are shifted towards control of inflation, reduction of government spending, and reduction of real wages.

In many industrial countries a tight monetary policy has been combined with efforts to reduce the tax burden and real wages so as to increase the profit share, but these attempts have not been very successful. First of all, any attempt to cut government spending programmes or to cut wages meets with fierce resistance from affected interest groups. As Mandel points out, the combination of such policies with a social democracy based on universal franchise does not result in a very stable political situation. But success has been limited even in economic terms. Cuts in government spending immediately lead to increases in unemployment and in payments of social security benefits; on the other hand, they lead to an income fall which is reflected in lower public revenues. As a result the tax burden hardly falls at all and the budget deficit remains high. Similarly, a fall in the rate of increase in nominal wages, if combined with a fall in the rate of inflation, may leave real wages almost unaffected; and when real wages fall, consumption demand is reduced.[26] The result is that the profit share does not increase and, even if it does, firms have little incentive to invest since the decline in government spending and in real wages leaves a very weak domestic demand for which to produce. If all major economies follow such a policy, moreover, foreign demand for export products will also be very low.

In conclusion, a generalised recession is hardly an efficient method with which to increase industrial profits. The negative demand-side effects of the policies will dominate and the expected positive supply-side effects will be very slow in

29

coming. Most monetarists admit this fact, but still argue that it is necessary to adhere to their policies so that, in the long term, the benefits may be reaped. The rigidities in the economic system, however (such as trade union wage negotiation practices; resistance against the disappearance of inefficient firms; difficulties in reducing government expenditure, and the budget deficit), may make that long term very long indeed. It was probably against this background that supply-side economics was formulated. Mundell supports the supply-siders in their claim for a tight monetary policy combined with an immediate supply-side incentive in the form of a considerable tax cut. Such a tax cut would be immediately felt by the firms as a cost reduction, and the resultant increase in economic activity should increase incomes to such an extent that the same tax receipts will ultimately be realised (a lower rate over a higher income). Ministers of finance, however, have not been convinced that this will be the case.

In addition to the failure so far to restore profits, the high rates of interest form another obstacle on the way to investment expansion. Opinions differ as to what causes the present high real rates of interest. Mundell and Heertje ascribe them to high inflationary expectations and do not expect them to decline until inflation has decelerated and inflationary expectations have been abated. Others ascribe the high rates to the tight monetary policy. Polak, however, blames the large budget deficit and the resultant substantial public sector borrowing for pushing rates of interest upwards. In his view, high interest rates are due not to tight monetary policy but to the loose fiscal policy. Others, including Kaldor, disagree with these views, considering that rates are high simply because the monetary authorities set the minimum lending rate at a high level and all other interest rates are calculated as a mark-up on that minimum [*Kaldor, 1980: 311*]. The importance of these debates, of course, is to determine whether rates of interest can be influenced by policy, and if so by what type of policy. Irrespective of the outcome of that debate, however, is the fact that the interest cost on debts of firms as well as governments has become very significant in recent years, while the high cost of lending has done little to stimulate private investment.

We have observed that investments in developing countries

are not so much profit constrained as foreign exchange constrained. The reduction in real wages introduced in some developing countries was thus needed to free foreign exchange by reducing consumer good imports rather than to increase the profit share. External borrowing has been another avenue by which levels of investment have been maintained. Here again, high interest rates and the resultant high debt servicing burden have caused great problems to several countries, not only in the Third World but, as Ellman points out, also Eastern European countries such as Poland and Romania. Jayawardena reviews some of the proposals that have been made for preventing such problems while still safeguarding the recycling mechanism.

Monetarism and the Balance of Payments

In theory, and often in practice, a monetarist control of the money supply is combined with a flexible rate of exchange. Under such a regime, a relative success in the struggle against inflation will lead to an appreciation of the exchange rate which, in itself, will contribute to a further deceleration of inflation.

This is good for inflation but what about the rest? As we have seen, the fight to reduce inflation and to restore profitability requires that domestic demand be controlled. Increases in production, employment and profits thus have to come from increased exports resulting from gains in international competitiveness. Under a flexible exchange rate regime those countries with a relatively good performance in the reduction of prices and production costs will see part of that gain in international competitiveness negated by an appreciating exchange rate,[27] which brings us face to face with the serious problem that in the present world economy monetarist policies do not immediately and fully reward the meritorious but, on occasion, may even punish them. The combination of differential rates of inflation, a high degree of mobility of capital, and flexible exchange rates, has left countries with far less policy-making autonomy than the theory of flexible exchange rates would lead one to expect.

Does this strengthen Mundell's case for fixed exchange rates? It seems that a fixed exchange rate system would also collapse quite quickly if the present difference between rates of inflation between major countries were to persist. Polak observes that reforms of the present international monetary system are blocked by lack of coordination and agreement among governments, and that we are thus stuck with the present imperfect system. Mundell expects the coordination of policies and policy discipline to result from an international system that is based on gold convertibility and fixed exchange rates, but it seems that the preconditions for such a system have not yet been fulfilled. Others, like Cripps and Jayawardena, suggest that agreement on monetary matters is not sufficient; above all, it is necessary that the unstable commodity markets should be coordinated.

The present international monetary system is clearly not helpful to the efforts made by industrial countries to overcome their crises. All countries try to increase their international competitiveness through deflation, but the net result is that they have to compete harder and harder for a market that is stagnating under their own deflationary policies. Given the volatility of exchange rates, it is not even certain that the country that makes the largest effort will indeed see its export share increase.

The developing countries, characterised by inconvertible currencies, pegged exchange rates, and rudimentary capital markets, face quite a different situation. Within the IMF Polak has developed an analytical model for such countries, known as 'the monetary approach to the balance of payments' [*IMF, 1977*]. The crucial variable in that model is domestic credit creation, an excess of which, given inelastic domestic supply or full employment, will lead to a balance of payments deficit. If a domestic capital market is lacking, excess credit creation is equivalent to excess expenditure. A balance of payments deficit can only be prevented by a halt to credit creation or by import control, but the latter will give rise to inflation. Thus the IMF concentrates its advice to countries with balance of payments problems or inflation on credit control. Little exception can be taken to this advice when the source of the disturbance is domestic, as it probably was in most cases prior to 1973. After that year, however, the balance of payments problems of most developing countries were external in origin: decline in the growth of volume of exports and increased terms-of-trade losses. When the shock is external, equilibrium on the balance of payments can only be restored through a painful domestic deflation, assuming for the moment that an expansion of exports is not feasible. It is then hardly surprising to find that, according to the IMF's own evaluation, success was achieved in three-quarters of all standby agreements in the period 1963-72, and that in the period 1973-75 the success rate dropped to one third.[28]

The IMF is aware of these problems. Recent articles written by IMF staff show some changes in thinking which may be summarised under three points [*Crockett, 1981; Keller, 1980; Khan & Knight, 1981*]. First, the control of domestic credit, and in general of domestic demand, remains a crucial factor. The emphasis on the need for undistorted internal and external prices is also maintained. Second, a preference is emerging for longer-term gradual stabilisation programmes rather than for short-term shock treatment. And third, there is a stronger emphasis on the supply-side of the economy, particularly on the effort to shift resources to investment and to export production. This shift is to be effected mainly through demand restraint and price liberalisation and, implicitly or explicitly, seems also to imply a shift of resources from the public to the private sector. This structural adjustment, the need for which is also stressed by Polak, is the major new element in IMF thinking. But two questions remain. First, can exports be increased? As Van Arkadie and others argue, a devaluation may be inflationary and a liberalisation of prices need not necessarily lead to the increased supply of export goods. The institutional reform of marketing arrangements and the provision of non-price incentives may be necessary steps which the market mechanism is unable to take. But even if the supply of export goods could be increased, could those goods be profitably sold?

The continued emphasis on policies to open up the economy, liberalise markets and promote exports seems to be caused by the success of a few countries that are alleged to have adopted such policies from an early stage. Their performance in terms of export growth, economic growth and employment is judged to be much better than that of other developing countries [*Balassa, 1981*]. It is also said that these countries have been better able to deal with the crisis of the 1970s in that their more diversified and flexible economic structures made it possible for them to reduce imports and to change their export composition without causing great shocks to the domestic economy [*Balassa & Barsony, 1981*]. The preferential access of these countries to the Euro-Currency market for credit has also been of help.

The danger of such comparative studies, however, is that they suggest more than they can prove. They claim that the success of these countries is due to the policies followed, and that other countries, almost irrespective of their past, their economic structure, their geographical location or their political conditions, could adopt similar policies and would meet with similar success. But what has been possible for a few countries need not necessarily apply to the greater part of the developing world unless, of course, proposals for structural adjustments in the Third World can be combined with their necessary counterpart: structural adjustment in the industrial countries. Until that time, efforts by developing countries to expand their exports are likely to encounter unfavourable markets, particularly under conditions of world depression such as apply at present.

A second question on the conditionality of the IMF which, according to Van Arkadie, is highly relevant in the case of Tanzania, is whether the basic message of the IMF to liberalise markets and to adjust a number of important relative prices, is compatible with government objectives with respect to income distribution and sectoral allocation. If not, has the IMF the authority to impose its view on its members?

CONCLUSION

One feature of the crises in capitalist development is that they allow a restructuring of production in which capital is shifted from old and relatively unproductive firms and industries to new and dynamic sectors. In the 1970s this restructuring took place not only between firms and sectors but also between countries. This is part of the internationalisation of the world economy, two aspects of which are particularly relevant here. First, the multinational corporations constitute large conglomerates of firms operating in various industries and in different countries; economic restructuring is thus, to a considerable extent, restructuring within the firm. Second, the increased international mobility of financial capital has made it easier to shift production capacity among sectors and among countries. There can be no doubt that such a restructuring of production among countries is in process, and is continuing during the current crisis. Some countries such as the UK are said to be de-industrialising, and in all industrial countries certain industries, e.g. textiles and shipbuilding, are in decline. A group of developing countries, labelled newly-industrialised countries, has emerged as the outcome of this process.

The economic crisis is accompanied by a notable shift in economic policy thinking – and, to a large extent, also in policy practice – towards monetarist-inspired policies. Few critics, and certainly none of those in this book, would see monetarist policies as the cause of the economic crisis, although some may maintain that these policies have deepened and lengthened the recession unnecessarily.

This is not a book about the theoretical assertions of monetarism, however, but about monetarism as an economic policy, and it is therefore relevant to ask whether monetarist-inspired policies have been able to supply an answer to the needs of our time.

The analysis given in the previous section can be summarised under five points.

(1) The success of monetarist policies in fighting inflation has so far been limited and slow in coming.

(2) Attempts to reduce the tax burden and the budget deficit in industrial countries have not met with success; if anything, the relative size of the public sector has increased in recent years. In the developing countries, the fact that the crisis had its primary effect on the balance of payments made it necessary for those countries with inconvertible currencies to take appropriate policy measures. In practice, many opted for the short-term solution of increasing their external indebtedness. These foreign loans are often channelled through the public sector and, in many cases, have increased the state control over resource allocation.

(3) In industrial countries, the wage share, like the tax

35

burden, did not decrease. Thus, profits and profit share remained low or fell further, preventing an investment recovery. In some developing countries at least, the wage share did fall, and together with external borrowing, allowed investment levels to be maintained. It should be noted that the larger share of public investment in total investment in developing countries as compared to the industrial economies, makes investment in the former less volatile. In both industrial and developing countries, however, investments have suffered from the high level of international interest rates.

(4) The flexible exchange rates for industrial countries did not create the autonomy for domestic monetary policy which the monetarists had expected. In many cases, moreover, it undermined attempts to improve the country's international competitiveness.

(5) In developing countries, monetarist policies were necessary to close the current account gap through domestic deflation. In quite a few, the need for domestic deflation was reduced by the ability to borrow internationally, and for some it was possible to close the gap through increased exports. This latter route was open mainly for those countries that already had an industrial base and export capacity, which could shift resources to export production, and could expand their share in export markets through cost advantages. But for the majority of developing countries which are new to industrial exports, this method is not very promising given the depressed state of world demand. Nevertheless, many of these countries have reacted to the international crisis by opening up the economy and by promoting exports. Three reasons can be suggested for such a reaction. First, the liberalisation of trade practices and prices would allow changes in international prices to be reflected in domestic prices so that the appropriate adjustments in consumption and production patterns could be made. Second, the economic crisis showed the limitations of the inward-looking development strategy thus far followed by many countries, and convinced some governments that the future growth of their country depended on increases in their exports. And finally, the access to international loans from commercial banks and the IMF as well as to direct private foreign

investment, requires an open policy outlook on the part of the receiving country.

These shifts in policy perspective have been presented variously as a liberalisation of the economy, as an opening up to market forces, and as a reduction of the role of the state. But is that so? In the developing countries an export-oriented policy needs a very clear and extensive role on the part of the state. Any significant restructuring of the economy – and this applies also to industrial countries – needs to be guided closely by state intervention and state support.

As such shifts in policy orientation imply significant changes in resource allocation and income distribution in the domestic economy, they presuppose – even when they are to a large extent forced by external factors – certain internal political relations and conditions. If these conditions are not met, opening up the economy will be impossible, although at the moment the alternative policy option is not clear.

It is impossible to avoid the conclusion that, in addition to the economic crisis, we also face a crisis in economic policy. The developments in the 1970s which made the conventional Keynesian policies irrelevant, ineffective and unpopular have already been identified. The shift to monetarist-inspired policies is clear; but have these policies been able to deal with the problems that Keynesian policies have failed to solve?

Ultimately, the solution of the economic crisis requires a revival of investments. In the industrial countries that revival will depend on three factors. First, an increase in profits to provide the incentives and finances for the investment. I have concluded that attempts to reduce real wages and government expenditure have not led to higher profits but rather to a deeper recession. A second condition for an increase in investment is a strong final demand. Domestic demand has been weak following attempts to control inflation, to reduce real wages and to cut government expenditure, and it is feared that stimulation of domestic demand may lead to inflation and to balance of payments problems. Attempts have been made to increase final demand through export growth, but as all industrial countries have followed a similar deflationary policy, world demand has been very weak. Third, investment needs a climate of stability

37

and confidence, which could be created by bringing inflation under control, and by establishing a more stable international monetary system with less variation in inflation rates between countries and with less volatile exchange rates.

In developing countries, investments are more dependent on import capacity. In the short run, the debt servicing burden has to remain within reasonable limits, but this is made difficult by high rates of interest. Ultimately, of course, import capacity is dependent on export earnings.

On all these counts, the performance of monetarist-inspired policies has so far been poor. Profits have not increased; policies have been deflationary without any clear positive effects; and stability and confidence seem as distant as ever. In short, progress has been unconvincing whereas the costs have been high. Failure is blamed partly on the political factors which have prevented the full implementation of the monetarist programme, but such political factors form part of reality.

It seems, therefore, that monetarism, as the conventional Keynesian alternative, is ineffective in the present economic situation. In the integrated world economy, national economic policies have lost much of their power to determine what should happen in individual countries, partly due to the fact that policy objectives have increased in number while the effectiveness of policy instruments has been reduced. It is perhaps inevitable that, when a crisis in a private enterprise industrial economy is really deep and fundamental, the power of public policy to deal with that crisis is much less than it was thought to be after the Keynesian revolution. But part of the crisis in economic policy is due to the fact that economic policy solutions continue to be formulated for the national economy, as though it still existed. National economies, however, now form part of an integrated world economy of multinational firms, and of internationalised commodities, capital and labour markets, and policy solutions have to be feasible in that context.

How should the crisis in economic policy be dealt with? This book brings together various suggestions. Mundell is in favour of supply-side incentives in an environment of stable currencies and fixed exchange rates. Cripps argues for expansion of domestic demand combined with import controls to deal with the consequences for the current account. He also argues for the international regulation of unstable commodity markets. Jayawardena presents the case for demand stimulation on an international scale through a transfer of purchasing power to the Third World in what could be called International Keynesianism. Strong arguments are also presented for a government-regulated restructuring of the economies of the developing world and also for some of the industrial countries by Seers, Jayawardena, Heertje, Van Arkadie and Polak. It is not the task of the editor to compare these various suggestions; it is for the reader to evaluate how far they provide an answer to the economic crisis.

NOTES

1. Whenever the name of one of the contributors to this book is used in this Introduction the reference is to his chapter in this book, unless a different reference is provided.

2. Temin [*1976*] argues that the money stock fell but that real money balances were held more or less constant. He attributes the fall in money stock to a decline in the demand for money rather than in the supply of money.

3. The tables included in this chapter are based on data from IMF: *World Economic Outlook*. The country classification used in that paper includes under 'industrial countries' the entire OECD with the exception of Greece, Portugal and Turkey. The 'oil exporting countries' cover the Gulf States and Indonesia, Venezuela and Nigeria. Of the non-oil developing countries, 'net oil exporters' include such countries as Bolivia, Congo, Egypt, Malaysia, Mexico, Peru, Syria, Tunisia. The group of 'major exporters of manu-factures' consists of Argentina, Brazil, Greece, Hong Kong, South Korea, Portugal, Singapore, Yugoslavia. And the 'low income countries' are Bangladesh, People's Republic of China, India, Kenya, Pakistan, Sri Lanka, Sudan, Tanzania and Zaire. The groups are rather uneven in size; whereas the 'major exporters of manufactures' have a population of roughly 260 million, the 'low income countries' count over two billion.

4. IBRD [*1981*] gives for the non-market industrial countries an average growth rate of 4.8 per cent over the period 1960-70 and of 5.2 per cent for the 1970s.

5. For data see IMF [*1981a: 114*] and OECD: *Main Economic Indicators* [*April 1982: 16, 17*].

6. OECD: *Economic Outlook [December 1978: 14*], shows that for OECD countries the growth of labour productivity declined sharply from the period 1964-73 to that of 1974-78. Leipziger [*1980*] gives data for the productivity decline in the USA in the 1960s and 1970s.

7. IMF [*1982*] and BIS [*1982*] show the deceleration of inflation in the last few years for the industrial countries.

Karel Jansen

8. Source IMF [*1981: 6*]. These data cover the medium and long-term debts of 87 non-oil developing countries. Table 5 *supra* shows only long-term debt of non-oil developing countries.

9. In the period 1975-80 the following countries were involved in such renegotiations: Chile, India, Turkey, Gabon, Peru, Zaire, Togo, Sudan, Sierra Leone, Liberia, Pakistan, Jamaica, Nicaragua [*BIS, 1982: 17*].

10. Real non-residential business investment in the USA, for example, had an average annual growth rate of 5.7 per cent in the period 1960-73, of 2.8 per cent in the period 1973-79, minus three per cent in 1980 and 2.5 per cent in 1981. Other major economies show similar decelerations in investment [*BIS, 1982: 28*].

11. This short summary follows closely the interpretation given in the most recent BIS report [*1982*] and may be taken as representing accepted economic opinion.

12. International reserves – defined as monetary authorities' holdings of SDRs, reserve position with the IMF, and foreign exchange, and excluding their holdings of gold – had a growth rate of 5.9 per cent over the period 1960-69 and of 19.6 over 1969-81. IMF: *International Financial Statistics*.

13. Cripps does not believe in the long-term trade promoting effects of a devaluation.

14. For a simple exposition of this model see Cripps & Godley [*1978*].

15. Various sources can be given on the fall in the rate of profit and profit share. Mandel [*1978*] gives a number of these. Hill [*1979*] finds for the OECD countries in the period 1955-75 no evidence of an increase in the rate of profit or profit share, and in quite a number of cases evidence of a decline. Rosenberg & Weiskopf [*1981*] provide us with growth rates for real after-tax net profits in the USA which varied from 6.2 per cent over the years 1954-65, to minus 0.6 per cent over the period 1965-73 to 1.3 per cent for 1973-79. Real after tax wages increased much more quickly in the latter two periods.

16. OECD: *Economic Outlook [December 1981]*.

17. Jansen [*1982*] gives some data for Kenya which support this trend, his data for Sri Lanka are less clear. In both countries the share of the public sector increased rapidly.

18. Balassa & Barsony [*1981*] give Brazil, Mexico, Peru and Portugal as examples of countries where external loans have failed to sustain investment.

19. In BIS [*1982*] the following negative effects of inflation are summarised: (i) it impairs economic efficiency as relative prices cannot do their allocative work; (ii) it penalises fixed income earners and creditors and in general encourages the struggle to maintain relative income positions; (iii) as rates of inflation will differ between countries and over years, uncertainty is increased.

20. It is interesting to remember that in 1970 Johnson attributed the rise and success of monetarism to the policy problem of 'inflation', for which Keynesian orthodoxy had no ready answer. Johnson did not then believe that monetarism would last as unemployment is ultimately a more important social problem than inflation. See Johnson [*1972: 50-69*]. History so far has not proved him right.

40

21. Cripps and his Cambridge Economic Policy Group colleagues argue that full capacity utilisation and new investment due to demand expansion will stimulate innovation, increase labour productivity and reduce real wage cost, and thus improve competitiveness; see for example, Cripps & Godley [*1978*].

22. For a discussion of the determinants of the size of the public sector see Jansen [*1982*].

23. Polak makes this assertion for the USA, the sources quoted in Note 7 above confirm it for the other industrial countries.

24. For a theoretical debate see Kaldor [*1980: 294*].

25. This is the position of Laidler [*1981*], and of Milton Friedman, and could be called the practical approach to fine tuning. The Radical Expectations variant of monetarism has recently attacked fine tuning, partly on theoretical grounds.

26. BIS [*1982: 30*] gives data showing that for the major industrial countries the wage share in total domestic factor incomes increased until the early 1970s, after which it remained stable until 1981.

27. See BIS [*1981*] which shows that some countries experience rate of exchange movements which undermine their efforts to increase their competitiveness. The high mobility of capital causes the rates of exchange to reflect the real economies, at best after considerable delay.

28. These data are drawn from Reichman & Stillson [*1978*] and Reichman [*1978*].

REFERENCES

Balassa, B., 1981, *The Newly Industrializing Countries in the World Economy*, New York, Pergamon Press.

Balassa, B. & A. Barsony, 1981, 'Policy Responses to External Shocks in Developing Countries', Paris, OECD.

Bank of International Settlements, 1982, *Annual Report 1 April 1981–31 March 1982*, Basle, June.

Cripps, F. & W. Godley, 1978, 'Control of Imports as a Means to Full Employment and the Expansion of World Trade: The UK's Case', *Cambridge Journal of Economics*, 2, 327-34.

Crockett, A. D., 1981, 'Stabilization Policies in Developing Countries: Some Policy Considerations', *IMF Staff Papers*, Vol. 28, No. 1, March, 54-79.

Hill, T. P., 1979, *Profits and Rates of Return*, Paris, OECD.

IBRD, 1981, *World Development Report 1981*, New York, Oxford University Press.

IMF, monthly, *International Financial Statistics*, Washington, IMF.

IMF, 1977, *The Monetary Approach to the Balance of Payments*, Washington DC, IMF.

IMF, 1981, *External Indebtedness of Developing Countries*, Washington DC, IMF, Occasional Paper No. 3, May.

IMF, 1981a, *World Economic Outlook*, Washington DC, IMF, Occasional Paper No. 4, June.

IMF, 1982, *World Economic Outlook*, Washington DC, IMF, Occasional Paper No. 9, April.

Jansen, K., 1982, *State, Policy and the Economy: with Case Studies from Kenya and Sri Lanka*, The Hague, Institute of Social Studies, Research Report No. 12.

Johnson, H.G., 1972, *Further Essays in Monetary Economics*, London, Allen & Unwin.

Kaldor, N., 1980, 'Monetarism and UK Monetary Policy', *Cambridge Journal of Economics*, 4, 293-318.

Keller, P.M., 1980, 'Implications of Credit Policies for Output and the Balance of Payments', *IMF Staff Papers*, September, 451-77.

Khan, M.S. & M.D. Knight, 1981, 'Stabilization Programs in Developing Countries: A Formal Framework', *IMF Staff Papers*, March, 1-53.

Laidler, D., 1981, 'Monetarism: An Interpretation and an Assessment', *The Economic Journal*, 91, 1-28.

Leipziger, D.M., 1980, 'Productivity in the United States and its International Implications', *The World Economy*, Vol. 3, No. 1, 119-34.

Mandel, E., 1978, *The Second Slump: A Marxist Analysis of Recession in the Seventies*, London, New Left Books.

OECD, twice yearly, *OECD Economic Outlook*, Paris, OECD.

OECD, monthly, *Main Economic Indicators*, Paris, OECD.

Reichman, T.M., 1978, 'The Fund's Conditional Assistance and the Problems of Adjustment, 1973-75', *Finance and Development*, Vol. 15, No. 4, 38-41.

Reichman, T.M. & R.T. Stillson, 1978, 'Experience with Programs of Balance of Payments Adjustment: Stand-by Arrangements in the Higher Tranches, 1963-72', *IMF Staff Papers*, June, 293-309.

Rosenberg, S. & T.E. Weisskopf, 1981, 'A Conflict Theory Approach to Inflation in the Postwar US Economy', *American Economic Review*, Vol. 71, No. 2, 42-7.

Rowthorn, R.E., 1977, 'Conflict, Inflation and Money', *Cambridge Journal of Economics*, 1, 215-39.

Temin, P., 1976, *Did Monetary Forces Cause the Great Depression?*, New York, W.W. Norton & Co.

II
The Origins and Evolution of Monetarism

by ROBERT MUNDELL

THE HISTORY OF MONEY

I am no longer as certain as perhaps I once was about what monetarism is, was, or will be. To trace the origins of monetarism is rather like tracing a river to its source, through its many tributaries and branches. There are various ways of approaching the origins of monetarism: the first is to see what has happened in the field of money and of monetary policies over the past years, decades or even centuries. Another is to trace the intellectual history of the development of monetary ideas over that period.

Monetarism can be conceived of as a body of ideas and practices which have inspired monetary policies since the very creation of money in ancient times; in other words, a body of thought associated with the implementation of monetary policies. The study of monetarism should start with the peoples of India, China and the Middle East who, five thousand years ago, enjoyed a monetary system. The Sumerians, the Chaldeans, the Chinese, the Indians and the Persians had monetary ideas. Coinage as we know it today is more recent, initiated by the ancient kings of Lydia, the forefathers of Croesus, who introduced the use of pure gold. Early coinages such as the dinar originated in India but spread quickly to Persia and the Middle East, and achieved prominence in the Moslem world through a gold coin minted at the end of the seventh century.

43

Western coinage in its recognisable form was introduced in the sense of a gold standard by Julius Caesar in 46 BC when he overvalued a coin that, under the name of solidus or bezant, survived until the sacking of Constantinople by the Venetians and the Crusaders in 1204 AD. The monetarist policies of Byzantium which were governed by the Court of the Sacred Trust, the origin of the modern Exchequer, were designed to ensure monopoly of the coinage, and of the profits from seigniorage with which the Empire financed its sway for many hundreds of years until the death of Frederick II in 1250 AD. Later, the Italian city states embarked on their individual gold coinages, giving birth to such important coins as the florin, ducat and sequin. Their example was soon followed by the emerging Atlantic powers starting with Portugal, then Spain, then Holland, France and England, and finally the last great Atlantic power, the United States. Britain moved on to a gold standard after 1717 when Sir Isaac Newton overvalued gold and thus reduced the role of silver. After European countries, including Holland and England, left gold in the late eighteenth century, Britain returned in 1819, maintaining it until 1931 except for the 1914-25 wartime suspension. From 1870 to 1914, the European gold standard – and I call it a European gold standard rather than an international one because it is often forgotten that 40 per cent of the world, mainly the Third World, was on a silver standard or on a satellite standard in that system – brought a period of glory to Europe when she was, as Max Weber put it, 'mistress of the world'. It was really a gold exchange standard, dominated by intrinsic gold coins of Europe and extrinsic currencies in the colonies, and combined with the emergence of joint stock banking systems. This grand epoch in civilisation was undermined by the upset in the balance of power when the continental hegemony of Germany was ensured, Japan rose as a great power in Asia and the USA assumed continental dimensions which rivalled the global power of the British Empire. The weakening of the British Empire after World War II, in conjunction with the eclipse of the Ottoman, Austrian and German Empires after World War I, laid the foundations for the political liberation of Africa and Asia in the post-war world and for the global hegemony and bipolarity of the superpowers: the USA and the Soviet Union.

By 1960, the emergence of the Sino-Soviet split and European recovery weakened the unity of the West, and the currency area under the aegis of the IMF and based on the dollar and its convertibility into gold at $35 per ounce, was undermined. The Bretton Woods system collapsed in 1971 when the USA gave up its explicit monetary leadership by abandoning convertibility, and the Europeans, hoping to create a European rival to the dollar, demanded gold at the under-valued price of $35 per ounce. The first attempts to achieve a European solution with a joint float against the dollar failed in 1973. Countries then assumed individual responsibility for their own inflation rates, with floating exchange rates, leaving the way open for the inflation of gold and oil prices, and for the flood of Euro-dollar liquidity. These two events, the breakdown of convertibility of the US dollar in 1971 (on which gold has always acted as the golden brake, governing the expansion of US money), and the breakdown of the fixed exchange rate system which had operated as a brake upon the monetary expansion of the other countries making up the system, gave way to a system which left the world's monetary systems unconnected to any metallic and intrinsic currency. There is thus nothing to prevent central banks all over the world from engaging in the progressive depreciation of their currencies against commodities. It is this post-World War II period that has laid the basis for what we think of as modern monetarism.

MODERN MONETARISM

The ideas of modern monetarism centre around the floating exchange rate systems of individual nations, without gold and no convertibility into the dollar or major currency. Under the monetarist doctrine each country is expected to chart its own course of inflation, the principal tool in this regard being control of monetary aggregates. This body of policy is closely identified with Milton Friedman who, perhaps more than any other, personifies the ideas that have spawned since the breakdown of the Bretton Woods gold exchange standard, and the economic crisis.

In 1976 the IMF introduced the so-called new monetary system which has a managed flexible exchange rate system, but this was nothing more than acquiescence to existing reality. The basic idea was to de-emphasise the importance and role of gold in the system, and to increase the role of the SDRs – the Special Drawing Rights – which had been agreed upon in 1967 and introduced in 1970 and, in fact, probably played a role in the break-up of the Bretton Woods system. *STOP*

Gold in fact is now more important than ever, and the instability of its price has exacerbated the economic crisis. To give some idea of the great changes that have occurred since 1971, in 1970 the value of gold reserves held by central banks in terms of dollars and valued at the official price of $35 per ounce, was about $37 billion. In January 1980, valued at free market prices, it had moved up to $600 billion. In other words, the value of gold reserves in the world went from $37 billion to $600 billion at the January 1980 price which was, of course, very high [*IMF, various months*]. This is close to a twenty-fold increase in the value of gold reserves. The nature of that change alone is awesome in comparison with the way people were talking in the 1960s about international monetary reform when an increase in international reserves of three or four billion dollars was thought to be a large amount. The first enactment of SDR was for $3.5 billion in 1970, three billion in 1971 and again in 1972, but since the floating of the gold price, increases to the tune of hundreds of billions of dollars have occurred. And not only the upward movement is significant, but also the fluctuations. Since January 1980 the value of the world gold stocks held by central banks has dropped dramatically from $600 billion to $345 billion [*Ibidem*]. At least part of the economic crisis with which we are faced in Europe today is due to the fact that external reserves have been sliced in half, leading everywhere to retrenchment policies.

START Not only the big increase in the value of gold stocks but also the increase in foreign exchange reserves has contributed to the growth of international liquidity. In 1970 foreign exchange reserves amounted to $45 billion, but in 1980 they were close to $300 billion, again a fantastic increase. But the whopper is the shift in Euro-dollar accounts which in 1950 totalled $10 billion, in 1960 $25 billion, in 1970 $163 billion; in 1981 they amounted to over two trillion dollars! [*Ibidem*]. This mushrooming of the two important ingredients of international reserves, i.e. foreign exchange holdings by central banks, and gold holdings at market prices, has been due to the breakdown in the discipline of gold as far as the United States is concerned, and the breakdown in the balance of payments discipline under fixed exchange rates in the case of the other countries.

This enormous expansion and the fluctuations of the gold price are the principal elements in creating the cycles and crises with which we are now familiar, and which are induced by the instability of the gold price and the instability of currencies since the introduction of the floating exchange rate system. In short, monetarism under the regime of Milton Friedman and his disciples has come to mean instability and excessive inflation, a breakdown of discipline both monetary and budgetary, because budget deficits are simply financed through inflation. It has led to disintegration not only within the Atlantic area but within European countries, because the instability and differential inflations of those countries have made it extremely difficult for Europe to achieve any of its monetary integration goals. Since 1973 the Europeans have become disillusioned with floating exchange rates and have sought refuge in a joint solution of monetary discipline. This began with the movement for a European currency. In 1969/1970 the initial phase of that movement broke down. The post-1973 experience with floating exchange rates, however, caused disenchantment with the idea that each individual country should establish its own monetary control and defend it against inflation through its own devices, and led to repeated attempts to re-create joint monetary control within the framework of a fixed exchange rate system inside Europe. So far, however, these attempts have had little success.

As a result of these problems, renewed interest has been shown in the intellectual and theoretical aspects of monetarism. My own contribution has been largely in developing the monetary approach to the balance of payments, the mix of fiscal and monetary policies, in the debate on the role of dominant currencies, and of optimal currency areas [*Mundell 1968; 1971*]. In my view, monetarists are people who want to use the currency as a means with which to enforce economic discipline and the economic harmony of policies. According to the monetary approach to the balance of payments, countries would fix their own currencies to a central reserve device and, through their own purchases and sales of reserves, would automatically determine their monetary policies. A fixed exchange rate regime is a monetary policy, and a country can only have one monetary policy. It either fixes its prices by setting a fixed exchange rate, or it fixes quantities, à la Friedman. The basic question is which is easier and which is more explicit. I am against Friedman's quantity rule because money changes its spots all the time. Definitions have to be changed from M1 to M2 and M3, M4 and M5 (and now in the USA M1a and M1b and M1c), adjusted for seasonal factors, and adjusted or not adjusted for savings deposits. Even more adjustments will need to be made whenever money changes its uses and financial innovations occur. Innovation cannot be stopped, and the monetarist rule therefore becomes a joke. Moreover, definitions take no account of Euro-dollar deposits which could be used for purchases of American goods.

It does not really matter what happens to the money supply. Not because money is not important, but because there are so many close substitutes for any definition of money, and new ones are constantly emerging.

SUPPLY-SIDE ECONOMICS

How can we find a way out of this crisis of unemployment and inflation? Three schools of thought are of significance in the United States: Keynesians, monetarists and supply-siders. In turn, these can be divided into many branches, because every economist has his own variation of what his particular school of thought reflects. But they can be grouped into the three dominant schools; first, the Keynesian school of fiscalists; and second, the Friedman school of monetarists. Some say that it is really Keynesianism divided into two halves. The Keynesian system was based on the intersection of an LM curve and an IS curve: the fiscalists took the IS curve to Harvard, and the Monetarists took the LM curve to Chicago. The third school is that of supply-side economics. This is the newest and least familiar of the schools, and it is therefore rather difficult to know exactly what it embraces. No less a person than the Vice-President of the United States has called it 'voodoo economics', although that was before he became a candidate for the Vice-Presidency. When Bush became Vice-President he had to conceal his opposition because many of the American President's economic advisers are supply-side economists.[1] I am also sympathetic to such views and have perhaps played a role in disseminating them. Economies that suffer from inflation and unemployment should find a solution to their economic problems not, as the monetarists insist, by creating a depression, but by adopting a mix of monetary and fiscal policies which will alleviate the need for a depression. According to the supply-siders, unemployment is not a factor that will help to stop inflation. In a recession the supply of goods and services is reduced, and a reduction in supply is *inflationary*, not deflationary. The object of any policy designed to stop inflation should therefore be directed towards the enhancement of supply.

The problem is how do you change supply differentially from demand? This can be done through the differential use of policies, in particular fiscal policies and monetary policies. Both the Keynesian fiscal and Friedman monetarist policies are demand-side policies. Until the time of Keynes, classical economics to some extent lacked any explicit aggregate demand schedule, and most writers on Keynes consider his most original and most important idea to have been the introduction of the aggregate demand schedule. It is certainly a major tool of analysis. Both Keynesians and Friedmanites concentrate on aggregate demand, and in both cases neglect the side of supply. The only way in which the supply side is affected in Keynesian analysis is through wage control or incomes policy. The Keynesians fix their attention on wage control or incomes policy rather than, like the monetarists, on floating exchange rates, largely because their work started at a time when floating exchange rates were not respectable and the world was by and large on the system of fixed exchange rates. Incomes policies thus became the way by which they could exert some kind of influence on supply. The Friedman monetarists, on the other hand, focus on the role of money supply, without any belief in wage control – they expect wages to be controlled over a longer period by unemployment which will cause wage demands to be reduced or at any rate moderated.

Supply-siders, on the other hand, reject the Friedman approach, holding the view that it makes the economy pay for halting inflation with a recession which will exacerbate the problem. In the USA, the big recession of 1969/70 was engineered by the Nixon Administration in order to reduce effective demand, and it was done through a very tight money policy. This was deliberate and was introduced by the Chicago-based task force immediately after Nixon's election. This policy was repeated after September 1974 by the brilliant alliance between Keynesians and Friedman monetarists, with their recommendation for an increase in taxes and for tight money, which created and exacerbated the recession of that year.

It was at that time that the supply-side school began to get established with its opposition to the tax increase that the then Secretary to the Treasury argued for. I was among those who at the time pressed for tight money to stop inflation, combined with a very large tax cut. Initially, in May 1974, I recommended a $10 billion tax cut, in August $20 billion, in November $30 billion, and then in December $60 billion, but the only result was the retention of the tax increase which had been planned by the Ford Administration in 1974. This was reversed in November 1974 and ultimately there was no tax change at all. It was not until April 1975 that a tax cut was introduced of $15 billion. This was not a supply-side-type tax cut, however, but a purely Keynesian-type cut, i.e. a rebate to consumers, not given in order to stress the incentive to produce, but purely a demand-based tax cut.

It was then that the Kemp-Roth Bill was introduced, which proposed a 30 per cent cut, i.e. 10 per cent in three consecutive years, in all income taxes. This was a major policy change which was largely put into practice after the election of President Reagan, but was watered down to a five per cent income tax cut in October 1981. Much delayed, unfortunately. I had recommended that it should be accelerated, from 10 per cent in three consecutive years, to 15 per cent in 1981 and again in 1982 to stop the expected recession. The best that the politics of the situation would tolerate, however, was a five per cent tax cut in

October 1981 followed by 10 per cent in July 1982, and another 10 per cent in July 1983. Much delayed and far too low, it meant that we have to pay the price of rising unemployment.

Most monetarists came to see the tax cut as a good part of the economic policy that had been put into effect, with some exceptions of course because the cost it entails is an increased budget deficit which some people find very worrying.[2] The alliance between the monetarists and the supply-siders against the Keynesians thus succeeded in gaining a tax cut. The shifts in government spending in the USA, including a reduction in the escalation of non-supply-based welfare programmes and a shift towards a stronger military defence posture, were also achieved by means of an alliance between the monetarists and the supply-siders within the administration. Subsequently, the major split emerged between the supply-siders and the monetarists over the role of gold and the movement back to a policy system which would ensure that future monetary policy would not simply be to float the exchange rate again, leading to further expansion of liquidity and engulfing the world in more inflation.

REQUIREMENTS FOR INTERNATIONAL STABILITY

The best way in which a return to international stability could occur would be through a return to some form of check on the expansion of the dollar and other currencies. How can this be achieved? Would it be possible, for instance, for such a new system to be based on SDRs?

The SDR began with a gold-weight guarantee of one thirty-fifth of an ounce of gold. On that basis the SDR was introduced in 1968 and the first allocation made in 1970. While it had a gold-weight guarantee, of course, it was clearly a substitute for gold which, in the economic system, had become the scarce element. As a result, after 1968 when gold was set loose in the free market, it did not go very far for the first three or four years. Even in 1970 gold did not shoot up very far, only starting to do so after the breakdown of the convertibility of the dollar into gold and after the SDR ceased to have a gold-weight guarantee. Without the linkage to gold the SDR became a substitute for the dollar. As a result, the price of gold then began to shoot up, reaching almost $200 an ounce in 1974, certainly after the second devaluation of the dollar and the floating of the European rates.

The lesson seems clear: an SDR cannot become a strong currency unless it has a constituency, and there is no political constituency for the SDR. A country without a currency is conceivable, but not a currency without a country. The same lesson applies to attempts to create a European currency, the ECU. In the long run you can have an ECU that is solid if there is a centralisation of monetary and even of fiscal policies within Europe. But such centralisation is only possible if there is a state, because the creation of a currency is and always has been the prerogative of a state with a government. And until the European governments move closer together it will not be possible for a new currency to become effective.

We have seen what happened when the Mitterrand government was elected – the French franc began to depreciate. Under the current plans for socialisation in France, moderate as they are and responsible as they have been, to a certain extent, any long-term hope of keeping the French franc in stability with other European currencies has to be ephemeral.

The important reality is that at the present time basic international reserves are constituted by dollars and gold. The beginning of the restoration of stability would therefore be to move to a system which in some ways would be similar to the Bretton Woods system which broke down in 1971, but without the undervaluation of gold that existed at that time. One thing is clear: until gold returns, the prognosis for the future is continued high interest rates because no one, even if they believe that tight monetary policies are a safeguard against inflation, will believe that governments will stick to tight monetary and fiscal policies.

Some day, when the Democrats come back to power perhaps, there may be a big budget deficit and a new spending spree and the US inflation rate will shoot up again to 10, 15 or 20 per cent a year, the price of gold will shoot up to $800 an ounce or maybe even $1000, and we shall be 'back at square one' in terms of stopping inflation. Gold is thus the only way in which continuation in policy lines can be ensured.

Similar results may be obtained for smaller countries by a return to the system of fixed exchange rates, because the targeting of the exchange rate is a monetary policy which allows the public to decide how much money should be available. What the fixed exchange rate will do is to set the compass to the polestar and show the rate of inflation that a particular country is going to experience. If a country fixes its currency to the dollar, it will eventually get the dollar rate of inflation, for good or ill. If the currency is fixed to gold, it will get gold's fluctuations; if it is fixed to the Deutschmark it will get the DM fluctuations. Milton Friedman himself, in talking about the less developed countries, has advised fixed exchange rates, because he thought that these would impose discipline on their monetary policies.

The alternative, floating exchange rates, leads to instability because political reasons can always be found for changing exchange rates. Political reasons, however, are almost never what they are said to be. They are usually connected with changing the relationship between debtors and creditors internally, but they are presented by academicians and other people as if they had something to do with making a country more competitive. Devaluation does not make a country more competitive. The exchange rate is not going to solve any of a country's real problems. The example of Chile is illustrative in this respect. After the Allende government, Chile went through a period of tight money and Friedman-type monetary control, with reduced money supply and resulting large-scale unemployment. Now that unemployment was not only due to the monetary policy followed. A large part of it was simply due to the fact that the whole world was suffering big increases in unemployment and, as a copper-producing country, Chile's difficulties in that direction were huge. But it was also due in part to the monetary disinflation policies adopted by the new regime. After initially following a policy of reducing the rate of monetary expansion, the government shifted away from the Friedman line onto a line that followed the monetary approach. The administrative objective was established as a change in the rate of depreciation of the exchange rate, the so-called Tablique system. Rates of exchange were indicated, and future rates were pegged with the scheduled depreciation of the exchange rate.

And whenever the Chilean regime moved away from that, whenever it lost reserves, the rate of monetary expansion was reduced or increased accordingly. Chile has now moved toward a fixed rate against the dollar and has brought inflation under control: for the past few months it has been zero or even negative. This is what fixed exchange rates and monetary discipline can achieve.

NOTES

1. The role of supply-side economists in the Reagan Administration is vividly described by Brooks [*1982*].
2. Later in 1982, President Reagan decided to *increase* taxes in order to close the budget deficit.

REFERENCES

Brooks, J., 1982, 'Annals of Finance: The Supply Side', *New Yorker*, 19 April.
IMF, various years, *International Financial Statistics*.
Mundell, R.A., 1968, *International Economics*, New York, Macmillan.
Mundell, R.A., 1971, *Monetary Theory*, Santa Monica, Cal., Goodyear Publishing.

III
What is Wrong with Monetarism?

by FRANCIS CRIPPS

A British economist invited to discuss the failings of monetarism might be forgiven for focusing on the effects of monetarist policy at the national level as witnessed, for example, in the UK where the adoption of monetary targets by the government has been followed by an unprecedented contraction of real output and employment. But my intention is to discuss what is wrong with monetarism in general and, more particularly, as it affects the international economy, because I believe that the international implications of monetarism are far more important than its consequences at the national level. I would attribute the things that have gone wrong in the UK and which are, to a greater or lesser extent, going wrong in other European countries and in the USA, above all to defects in the international economy as a system, because national economic policy at least in Europe is tightly constrained by international developments. Therefore, the central issue of economic policy in this decade and perhaps the next is how to have better management of the world economy in order to permit sustainable patterns of development for the economic systems in different parts of the world. As it is now, the chances of an adequate or acceptable path of economic and social development in most parts of the world are exceedingly poor. The set of ideas which I shall describe as being monetarism is to quite a considerable extent responsible for the failure to change the world system in any constructive manner.

Francis Cripps

THE PROPOSITIONS OF MONETARISM

I shall assume that the term monetarism refers to belief in two propositions which are distinct but related to one another. The first is that the availability of finance (or the money supply or the circumstances of money supply) affects the general level of prices in an economic system but does not affect the real economy, by which is meant the level of employment, the productivity of the production system, the pattern of income distribution, and so on. This is the most familiar proposition of modern monetarism. The other proposition which is just as important is that the real economy (the level of employment, productivity, the pattern of income distribution and so on) is, or should be, determined by the laws of free competition. As I shall now argue, there is a close connection between these two propositions, the one about the money supply and inflation, and the other about competition and the real economy.

Probably the most important theorem of modern economics is that which states that a pure competitive equilibrium will yield an optimum distribution of products, the best possible allocation of resources, and the most efficient choice of production techniques. This theorem is known in the academic literature as the Pareto-optimality of general equilibrium. It is the kernel of modern economic theory; more than that, it is a vision which inspires a large number of economists, especially those coming from the other side of the Atlantic who grew up in a society where competition seemed to have been the key to achievement of a high level of prosperity. In the theoretical vision of the pure competitive economy, one flaw is admitted by all, namely, that nothing can be said about the justice or otherwise of the distribution of income which may result. But this flaw is not enough to destroy the vision. Now it is easily shown that the allocation of resources and choice of techniques in the state of general equilibrium with perfect competition depends only on relative prices. All decisions about the real economy, what to produce and what to consume, depend on the ratios of prices. They have nothing to do with the price level. Evidently, although there is a substantial problem about how it could happen in practice, the pattern of prices required in order to

56

produce the general equilibrium of the competitive system ought to depend only on the conditions of the real economy – upon what technologies are available, what real resources exist, what consumer tastes are, and so on. In all of this there is no role for money. Money should have no relevance whatsoever to the equilibrium of the real economy. If somehow money did have an important relevance to the real economy, a lot of doubt would be cast on the optimality of the competitive equilibrium.

The role left for money within the general equilibrium system is to determine the overall price level. Money is a numeraire and the price level can be regarded as the same thing as the relative price of money. If there is more money its price will probably be lower relative to other prices. If there is less money its price will probably be higher. It is this deduction or intuition which leads most economists who wish to believe in the vision of the optimum production and distribution of goods and services in the real world being achieved through pure competition to believe also in the proposition that the supply of money determines the price level without in any way distorting the equilibrium of the real economy. It is therefore no accident that the two propositions of monetarism, the one about the efficiency of competition and the other about the money supply only affecting the price level, go together. Economists who subscribe to the one without the other are in a fundamental sense being inconsistent.

MONETARISM AS AN IDEOLOGY

It is not only in the academic world that the two propositions are normally combined. The idea of the separation between money and inflation on the one side and what happens in the real economy on the other is a valuable ideology for the banking and financial system. It allows bankers to disclaim responsibility for unemployment and for economic inefficiency. Whatever goes wrong in the real economy can be ascribed to imperfections of competition in markets for real resources and products. The clear, but limited, responsibility of the financial system, according to monetarism, is one of ensuring 'sound money'. We need sound money to avoid inflation and maintain a stable price level. It is perhaps an historical accident that bankers have been able to subscribe so wholeheartedly to monetarist propositions during the last decade. The inflation which has occurred could be blamed on national governments through the argument that it was the financial requirements of governments which obliged banks to create unsound money. If governments had meticulously balanced their budgets during the past decade bankers would have been in a different situation. It would then have been harder for them to endorse the doctrine that it is the supply of money that creates inflation because they would have been pointing the accusing finger at themselves.

Another field in which monetarism is important is politics. Monetarism has been a convenient doctrine for laissez-faire politicians – those who wish to see the state play a minimum role in society. The reason why monetarism has been so popular among these politicians is, in my opinion, that the case for reducing the functions of the state in modern society is extremely ambiguous. The case became compelling and electorally successful only when a reduction in the role of the state could be presented as a financial necessity. The most convincing argument to the public at large has been that our societies cannot afford high public expenditure because this leads either to excessive taxation or to inflation caused by governments printing money. Thus monetarism has offered laissez-faire politicians a ready-made explanation of why it is important to cut down the role of the state in contemporary society.

THE FUNDAMENTAL ERROR OF MONETARISM

Monetarism rests on an error which unfortunately underlies a great part of modern economics. The error concerns the manner in which markets operate, or could operate, in a modern society. The fiction at the centre of the theoretical construction is the idea that we have (or should have or nearly have) an economic system in which prices provide the main signals which determine how economic agents behave, with prices being set in such a way as to bring the system as a whole into an equilibrium in which markets are cleared and resources are not wasted. The truth is that in modern economies prices play only a small role in clearing markets for the good reason that competitive fixing of prices to clear markets is a highly unstable

58

process. There are a few markets in our society which are genuinely cleared by prices – stock markets, foreign exchange markets (in the absence of regulation and intervention) and a small number of markets for commodities such as wheat, cotton, rubber and certain metals. The outstanding characteristic of all these markets which are cleared by price is that they are unstable and that prices are highly unpredictable. These markets have become a kind of gambling forum, the unpredictability of prices making them a medium for speculation.

In the history of the modern economic system as it has evolved over the past 150 years a wide variety of mechanisms evolved for regulation of different kinds of markets. Nearly all these mechanisms of market regulation involve restriction of price competition and its replacement by some form of conventional pricing behaviour, of which the most typical and widely-discussed is normally referred to as mark-up pricing – the practice whereby leading producers assess the normal cost of production of a product, add a percentage for profit, and judge that as being the reasonable price. There are of course other forms of price determination in different markets. For example, in the labour market the normal way of determining price (in this instance the wage) is influenced by social norms about the life-style and status of the people doing the work. The restriction of price competition and its replacement with conventional pricing behaviour has been responsible for a high degree of stability in most prices in modern economies, especially as regards their relativities one to another. So far from living in a world where relative prices are changing all the time so as to provide signals for markets to be cleared, we live in a world where relative prices change only slowly. Markets have to be cleared in other ways. Some are cleared by queues, that is, by having order books. The majority of markets are typically cleared by having a margin of excess supply capacity which allows producers to adjust the volume of supply to the volume of demand. Another group of adjustment mechanisms operating simultaneously is described by economists under the label of non-price competition. These adjustments typically take the form of product competition, with producers trying to improve products or differentiate them or market them in more attractive ways. There are also certain parts of the production process where market relationships as such have almost entirely been displaced, being internalised within large firms where production is coordinated by directive planning procedures.

All these different patterns that exist for the regulation of markets which organise production and distribution must, in general, have two kinds of properties to be functional in the modern economic system. One, which is conventionally emphasised and which is indeed very important, is flexibility so that the economic system can adapt to take advantage of widening technical possibilities and respond to changes in the availability of resources. The other, which needs emphasis in a critique of monetarism, is that market arrangements must provide stable conditions for production and distribution. It is the stability of markets for products and labour which has permitted modern societies to make huge investments which would otherwise have been exceedingly risky. Such investments not only in fixed capital but also in research and development and, perhaps more important still, in training and highly specialised work experience, have been the main source of the extraordinary increases in productivity, real income and standard of living which our society has enjoyed during the past century. Modern life as we know it could never have evolved, and could not continue in everyday operation, if markets really had to conform with laws of perfect competition, clearing through price adjustments alone.

THE CONCEPT OF AGGREGATE DEMAND

Fifty years ago Keynes employed the concept of aggregate demand to explain why market economies may suffer long periods of gross under-utilisation of resources. Unfortunately Keynes chose a form of exposition which retained many conventional assumptions, including the view that product markets are cleared by price. The proposition which Keynes thought he had proved has been the subject of prolonged controversy because his analysis can easily be modified to yield very different conclusions.

The point that Keynes made is more obvious and general if the analysis of demand is conducted in the framework of a model of the economic system which recognises that most markets are cleared chiefly by adjustment of the volume of supply rather than by the price mechanism. For it is then clear that at any moment of time there is a unique value for aggregate purchasing power in money terms which would be sufficient to purchase the full-employment volume of output; if money purchasing power exceeds this value there will be shortages and other symptoms of 'over-heating' while if money purchasing power falls short there will be wastage of resources and production capacity.

There is not too much dispute in the economics profession about what governs the level of aggregate purchasing power (except at the level of technical detail). Whether a low level of purchasing power is described as being the result of a shortfall in credit creation relative to demand for financial assets or whether it is described as being the result of low investment relative to saving makes little difference. The essential problem is one of people seeking to hold too much money or other forms of financial wealth, being unwilling to borrow or spend enough on purchases of goods and services.

The conclusion which has to be drawn is that, if a modern economic system is to function properly, a mechanism is required for the management of aggregate demand. Now it happens that the need for management of aggregate demand within a closed national economy can be met rather easily. It is easily met because national economies have an institution called the state which is unique in that it has virtually unlimited powers of credit creation or borrowing (or would have within a closed national economy). Keynesians gave up at this point, thinking that once the need for demand management had been pointed out, and the possibility for demand management by a national government had been understood, the problem of demand management was solved once and for all. Unfortunately, there is no such thing as the state in the contemporary international economy at the international level and the absence of the state as such at the international level is, I believe, a sufficient explanation of why the world economy has run into serious problems of recession.

It could not have come at a worse time that we suffered the monetarist counter-revolution against Keynesianism. Monetarism has confused everybody by denying the need for demand management in relation to the problems of under-utilisation of capacity and employment and has confined the role of money creation (that is borrowing by the state or other institutions) to the determination of inflation and the price level. The other proposition of monetarism has been just as unfortunate, for the doctrine that allocations in the real economy should be determined by perfect competition has obstructed the search for alternative solutions to the international demand management problem in the absence of world government.

THE GLOBAL RECESSION

I want to emphasise first that the monetarist counter-revolution has not ended attempts at demand management by national governments. Some people attribute the world recession mainly to manifestations of monetarism at the national level. It is said that there are too many monetarist governments deflating demand in their own countries and that is why we have an international recession. But strictly monetarist approaches at the national level, although no longer exceptions, cannot yet be regarded as the rule. They are generally referred to as experiments. France had the Barre experiment, the UK has nearly finished the Thatcher experiment, the US has started the Reagan experiment and I do not know the name of the German experiment to come. But the Barre experiment, the first really important one in Europe, was followed by the Mitterrand reflation and it is still far from clear that monetarism has been established as the norm for demand management policies by national governments.

The important point is rather that in an international economy the possibilities of national demand management are strictly limited. They are limited by problems of balance of payments adjustment and international finance. Governments that wish to regulate national demand so as to sustain full employment run into problems of increasing trade deficits and, in economies with liberal exchange regimes, loss of confidence and outflows of capital. It is actual or potential balance of payments crises which have been decisive in breaking the habit of Keynesian demand management at the national level. Many national governments are still trying, but they are trying under difficulties and they are frightened of balance of payments problems that would result if they tried too hard.

Now if the problem of the balance of payments is a constraint on national demand management, we have to look for ways of overcoming this before there can be a general increase in demand and better regulation in the international economy as a whole. This issue has been much discussed in recent years and several different solutions can be envisaged. One approach to easing balance of payments constraints in the international economy is to increase the amount of credit creation with the aim of generating more finance for trade deficits to match the trade surpluses and asset accumulation which occur whenever the world economy achieves a suitably high level of activity and an adequate rate of economic growth. But this is not the only approach. Another approach, which is also much discussed, is to try to improve mechanisms of balance of payments adjustment so as to make the level and rate of growth of demand in national economies less rigidly tied to one another and to permit the achievement in general of more adequate growth rates without giving rise to large imbalances in trade and international payments. There are some solutions which lie between the two – for example, ideas of seeking a pattern of long-term direct investment and capital flows which would contribute both to a monetary solution, by improving world credit creation, and to a structural solution by changing the trends of trade.

In respect of the two main lines of attack on the problem, the twin propositions of monetarism have played an important and exceedingly negative role. The doctrine of sound money is used to encourage credit restriction, not credit creation at the international level. The idea that it would be a good thing for the world economy if more countries incurred trade deficits and borrowed more (in particular if their governments borrowed more) is something which is not in vogue at all and has not been during the past decade. Thus, the magnificent contribution of the United States in stabilising the world economy in the late 1970s when the USA began to run very large balance of payments deficits was not much appreciated by anybody and the equally heroic deficits incurred by European countries in the aftermath of the second oil price increase have been short-lived because they were not regarded as being the necessary and virtuous counterpart of surpluses generated in other parts of the world trading system by a high level of economic activity.

It is not only the doctrine of sound money which stymies constructive thinking about how to get out of international recession. The other aspect which is just as important is the need for more quick-acting and reliable techniques of balance of payments adjustment. Instruments for balance of payments adjustment are severely restricted by the doctrine that free or purely competitive markets provide the optimum allocation and distribution of real resources. The doctrine of free markets strongly discourages government intervention in trade and capital flows. It leaves only one permissible mechanism for the regulation of trade balances – that is, changes in the exchange rate and/or domestic price or wage level. The only 'pure' way to overcome a balance of payments deficit is to procure a devaluation of the exchange rate or a cut in money wages so as to make the economy which is in deficit more competitive. At the same time, the doctrine of free markets, applied to capital markets, actually makes exchange-rate adjustment exceedingly problematic. Free capital markets are potentially unstable and governments which adopt medium-term policies of devaluation risk speculative attacks on their currencies which can cause very uncomfortable situations to develop such as that suffered in Europe by Italy earlier in the 1970s and by the United Kingdom in 1976 when interest differentials of eight or nine per cent were incapable of preventing continued capital outflows on an already undervalued exchange rate. The fear of crisis which has been inculcated in governments by free capital markets makes them reluctant to resort at all strongly to the exchange rate as an adjustment mechanism. And the fear of being labelled interventionist makes then unwilling to resort to other types of balance of payments adjustment through planning and intervention in trade. Thus, monetarism has blocked off international credit creation and it has also blocked off all mechanisms for balance of payments adjustment except wage cuts.

NON-MONETARIST SOLUTIONS

In my view it is tempting but wrong for economists in the Keynesian tradition to wish to resurrect the idea of demand management by some kind of world authority. The political background to the breakdown of the Bretton Woods system and the whole experience of trying to operate a highly coordinated international monetary system with exchange rates being decided officially by negotiation shows the limitations of relying on a world monetary authority. In the absence of a world monetary authority, while we may all seek to encourage countries to go into debt whenever they can and support the development of banking institutions that would make it easier for them to do so, we must recognise that credit creation in the world economy is at best going to be a fairly haphazard affair. That means that we must have better mechanisms for adjustment of the balance of payments if we are to have hopes of higher levels of economic activity and growth.

There are different analytical approaches to the question of balance of payments adjustment. But any realistic approach must take account of how different markets are actually regulated. We need to understand not only how trade balances might be adjusted more readily, but also why trade balances get out of adjustment in the first place. If economists could remove blinkers that say that all markets are more or less competitive and look at the structure of particular markets, they might reach useful conclusions about real life sources of trade imbalance and what could be done about them.

THE ENERGY MARKET

I want to take two examples which are important now and will remain so for a long time to come. The first is the energy market which has been a fundamental source of imbalances in trade since the early 1970s. At the moment the energy market is easily the most important single product market in the world. The money value of energy use in the last few years calculated at oil-equivalent world prices is something like 10 per cent of the money value of total final expenditure and income. I doubt whether any other product has achieved a comparable importance in modern economic history. Before 1973 the international energy market was regulated by a cartel that was popularly known as the Seven Sisters. It was a cartel of major international oil companies which more or less stabilised the world price of oil and thereby set the main price which other energy sources had to try to meet. In 1973 the old cartel was replaced for understandable reasons by a new cartel, OPEC. But the new cartel, instead of receiving aid and cooperation in its task of regulating the world energy market, met considerable hostility and attempts at destabilisation on the part of the West. The effect of this change and of the underlying argument about the legitimacy of the new cartel has been that OPEC has found it exceedingly difficult to stabilise energy prices and has failed to provide a secure framework for the development of the world energy sector. This has the consequence that imbalances in energy trade have been unstable and difficult to foresee. Instead of there being a planning framework within which countries might have progressively adjusted their energy imbalances or worked out the degree to which in the long run they would have to offset them by specialisation in other branches of trade, governments and companies have remained uncertain of what to do. They have hoped, on the one side that the price of oil would fall, on the other side that it would stay high. The imbalance of energy trade remains an unresolved issue which, if there is an upturn in the world economy, will immediately spring back to the centre as an obstacle to the sustaining of any recovery from world recession.

Monetarism has not encouraged us to see the need for regulation of the world energy market. But I do not think that there could be a solution to balance of payments problems at the global level without a more stable energy market within which long-term planning of the energy sector might be secured.

INDUSTRIAL MARKETS

Another obvious long-standing cause of balance of payments problems has been world industrial markets. It is well known that ever since the early days industrial production has always tended to develop selectively, concentrating in comparatively small geographical areas which then become highly populated and urbanised, being distributed unevenly within as well as between countries. The tendency towards concentration of industrial development remains pronounced in the modern world and is as true of the growing poles of new industrialisation as it was in the traditional centres of industry. We now have a system of regulation of world industrial markets through transnational companies and various types of oligopolies. This system of regulation has its main focus on the development of products and technology, on the reduction of costs of production, and on the extension of markets. It is not very much concerned with securing an even distribution of industry between countries and areas. So the pattern of industrial growth goes on being a source of divergent balance of payments trends. There may be a real dilemma because in some respects the mechanisms of global industrial markets have been exceedingly successful. There is no doubt that they have, on the whole, succeeded in promoting rapid technical development and they have achieved very considerable rates of technology transfer. But that still leaves the unresolved problem of how to regulate the distribution of industry between countries and areas. This, together with the energy problem, is a dominant source of persistent balance of payments problems. Once again, the contribution of monetarism has been completely negative because its only prescription is the dogmatic and unrealistic assertion that price signals ought somehow to do the job – that is to say, that exchange rate changes and changes in money wage levels between countries should somehow, if properly done, bring the distribution of industry around the world into a more balanced state.

Since exchange rate and money wage changes have in practice consistently failed to secure a balanced geographical distribution of industry, the monetarist prescription is hollow. The task for economists today ought to be first of all to understand how systems of regulation in the main markets of the world cause problems of balance of payments adjustment, and then to consider how those systems of regulation might be modified, through state intervention and other means, so as to permit a more effective adjustment process to take place. Until the economists in our society get around to tackling this problem, we risk being stuck with long periods of world recession, even if we are occasionally and accidentally favoured with periods of world boom.

IV
Monetarism: Is the Debate Closed?

by ARNOLD HEERTJE

INTRODUCTION

The question in this title about whether or not the debate on monetarism has been closed can be answered with a very simple 'No!'.

There is no agreement about the role of money in Western and Third World economies or, therefore, about monetarism at the theoretical, the empirical, or the policy level. After studying the other contributions to this book, and after re-reading the theoretical literature on monetarism, I have come to the conclusion that I should concentrate here on the significance of monetarism for the shaping of economic policy. In doing so, I am unable to do justice to the many interesting and subtle discussions between, for example, Friedman and Tobin, and Friedman and Galbraith, and also among the members of the monetarist family. These continuing discussions undoubtedly enrich economic theory, but the basic foundations for present-day monetarist policies can be understood without a detailed description of the modern theory of money. Moreover, there is strong evidence that the actual application of monetarist ideas in real life is largely independent of the outcome of the often very refined theoretical arguments and debates.

For central bankers, monetarism boils down to Friedman's famous rule that the monetary authorities have to keep the growth rate of the stock of money within limits so that only a real and not a nominal increase of national income will be

69

financed. The theoretical background to this rule is the insight that, in the end, inflation is a monetary phenomenon. Too big a monetary expansion is the root of an increase in the absolute level of prices. Demand pull and cost push are nice words to describe how a price increase comes about, but the price increase itself needs the availability of newly-created money to be realised.

The simple identification of inflation and an increase of the price level has for a long time detracted attention from the monetary aspects of the inflation process. From a monetary point of view, there is no difference between a change in the stock of money below or above the full employment level of the economy, although below that level output will increase and above it prices will increase. It is not without some pride, therefore, that I make passing reference to the fact that in my textbooks since 1961, I have adopted the monetary interpretation of inflation and deflation, and I shall not change this.

It could, of course, be argued that inflationary pressures are in fact due to wage increases which are bigger than the rise in productivity, and to public expenditure that is not properly balanced by public revenue. And from this one is inclined to conclude that an incomes and price policy is needed to establish equilibrium between wages and productivity, and that fiscal policy is needed to get rid of monetary financing in the public sector. It does not seem necessary to emphasise here how, in the 1960s and 1970s, incomes, price and fiscal policies failed to bring inflation under control.

For many years now we have been confronted on a national and on a world-wide scale with inflation and unemployment. Inflation will continue in the form of an increase of the absolute level of prices, as long as the monetary authorities provide the system with the liquidity needed to establish an imbalance between expenditure and income in the public and private sectors. The expectation of ever higher prices will become a permanent feature of the economic and social situation. As soon as the monetary authorities refuse to provide the system with the necessary liquidity to finance nominal increases of income and production, the inflationary process may be stopped, first by bringing down inflationary expectations and then by bringing down inflation itself. In the short run we are faced with serious social costs. Tensions in the political sphere, due to the necessity for governments to restrict public expenditure in a period of an already deteriorating economy. Tensions on the labour market between labour unions and employers' organisations, and a further rise in unemployment. But in the long run a lower rate of inflation and therefore of the rate of interest will emerge, both of which seem an absolute necessity if the economy is to be cured and the unemployment problem solved.

THE POWER OF CENTRAL BANKERS

In our modern Western economies we have learnt that the structure of the political process hampers implementation of the proper set of policy measures needed to stem inflation and therefore unemployment in time. The full burden of the struggle for a stable price level then lies in the hands of the central banks which, in principle, are able to stop the creation of inflationary ammunition.

But the question I would like to ask now is, is it really true that central bankers are able to refuse the creation of new money? Not always. In some countries the central bankers are public officials who belong to the Ministry of Finance. They then have a dependent position and are inclined to obey orders. In such cases, central bankers are part of the political process, characterised either by the permanent necessity to negotiate with political parties, pressure groups and individuals, of which the outcome is always that they do less than is necessary, or by dictatorship where they do more than is preferable. Such countries, for example, Indonesia, Israel and many countries in South America, experience very high rates of inflation in the order of perhaps 100 or 150 per cent.

The other situation is where central bankers have an independent position, as in the United States, Germany, Switzerland and The Netherlands, and where they make use of their power position. In these countries, rates of inflation are much lower than in those where central bankers have a dependent position, where in fact they are civil servants and behave as civil servants. It is thus a matter of the institutional structure and of the way in which it is used.

Arnold Heertje

This point is in my view of the utmost importance. The economic theory of the political process and democracy has provided us with the insight that the behaviour of politicians may be better explained by the hypothesis that they aim at some specification of their own interest rather than at the general interest. Their own interest is often to be re-elected. Civil servants also aim at their own interest, for example they like to obtain higher budgets from the central or local governments. These hypotheses may explain why the measures that have to be taken are not carried out in time and on a sufficient scale. If the central banker's position is structured so that he does not have to take popularity or re-election into account in his actions, his behaviour may and can be more in line with considerations of general interest. In The Netherlands, for example, the position of the President of the Central Bank relative to the government has been laid down in the Banking Act of 1948 in a very subtle and wise way. It would be disastrous if that position were changed so that the President would be more dependent on policies carried out by the Ministry of Finance. Volcker in the USA also has a very strong position and continues to make use of it. Despite criticism by the Reagan Administration and by European countries, he continues with his very tight monetary policies along the lines of the monetarist approach. He has restricted credit so that the nominal rate of interest has become higher than the rate of inflation, which is an essential step to bring inflationary expectations and inflation down.

If we think about the effects of the application of the Friedman rule in those countries where central banks have a strong and independent position, we can only conclude that, as regards inflation, their policies are successful, despite the internationalisation of banks and the increased diversity of financial assets. One reason may be that the central bankers concerned, being so few, are very effective in their tacit cooperation.

RESULTS OF MONETARIST POLICIES

It is necessary to adhere to monetarist policies for a certain period in order to get results. As long as the rate of interest remains below the rate of inflation, even though at a high level in absolute terms, inflation will continue and will increase. The paradox here is that to reduce the rate of inflation in the long run, and therefore also the rate of interest, it is necessary to start with very high levels of rate of interest. If this is lowered prematurely, the end result will be that inflation continues and the interest rate level will rise again.

To illustrate the success of Volcker's tight monetary policy, let me remind you that the rate of inflation in the USA, over a period of about two years, dropped from 18 per cent to roughly five per cent. There is a great deal of criticism of the monetarist approach as it is applied by the central banks in the USA and, for example, Great Britain. But I am convinced that the policy will prove successful. It is argued that it takes too much time, and that the price in the form of massive unemployment is too high. It is true that it takes time to get rid of inflation. But it should not be forgotten that we have been pursuing inflationary policies since the early 1960s, and that only recently have we introduced a strong anti-inflationary policy based on the monetary weapon. Furthermore, it is due to the failure of other policy measures that monetary policy has to bear the full weight of anti-inflation policies and therefore has to be even more severe than would otherwise have been the case. The price of huge unemployment is indeed very high, and the serious drawbacks for those who lose their jobs should not be under-estimated. The psychological, medical and political consequences of unemployment have so far been given far too little consideration. Without the strong approach now being applied, however, the situation would become even worse in the long run. The total collapse of the private and public sector in the light of continuing high rates of inflation and interest would cause rates of unemployment that would be far higher than those to which we are now accustomed, with all the attendant dangers for our economic, social and political systems.

The importance of bringing down interest rates through a diminution of the rate of increase of the price level, can hardly be over-estimated. This is a very effective method with which to get the recovery of the economy under way, given the enormous range of technological potential that awaits commercial exploitation. A lower rate of interest will have a direct positive impact on the economic activities of consumers and producers, and will improve the budget position of the public sector. Against the negative attitude shown with regard to developments in the USA and Great Britain, I wish to express my view that in the coming months a decline in the rate of interest will prove to be the starting point for improvement of our economic situation and also, therefore, the unemployment situation. I consider this to be the result of the monetarist policy followed by central bankers who have acted in the spirit of the Friedman rule.

It seems to me that, in The Netherlands too, the central bank is achieving success in bringing down the rate of inflation by adapting Friedman's rule. For a long time the rate of interest has been relatively high, partly due to protection of the external exchange rate of the guilder. This has helped to bring inflation down and has restricted the financial means available to those who otherwise would have prolonged their inflationary behaviour in the private and the public sectors.

A striking factor is the high rate of real interest, i.e. the difference between the nominal rate of interest and the price level. Apart from lack of confidence that the decline in the rate of inflation will be permanent, I am inclined to think that the 'black' or unofficial economy plays a role here. If the authorities determine the future increase in the stock of money on the basis of official figures on production, investment, consumption, etc., while in fact money disappears through non-official channels, a tightening in the official money market takes place which has an adverse effect on the rate of interest. In this way, the actual rate of interest may be two per cent higher than would have been the case without the unofficial or underground economy.

MONETARISM AND SUPPLY-SIDE ECONOMICS

Application of the Friedman rule in the sense of a rule regarding central bank behaviour in the sphere of monetary policy, should be carefully distinguished from so-called supply-side economics. The idea of strengthening the growth potential of an economy through tax incentives and a better climate for private investment, has nothing to do with monetarism. A contradiction might even be constructed, at least in the short run, between strict application of the principles of monetarism and supply-side economics. Excessive high rates of interest are not very helpful in the stimulation of investment, which is one of the elements in a supply-side programme. After some time, however, interest rates may come down so that monetarism and supply-side economics become consistent, although still representing different sets of policy measures, with different theoretical foundations.

MONETARISM IN THE NARROW AND THE BROAD SENSE

The defence and adaptation of Friedman's rule in the sphere of central banking so far, does not oblige us also to accept the other parts of his message. In particular, Friedman's idea that application of his rule not only is necessary to restore balanced growth and full employment, but that it is also sufficient. The theoretical background of his position is that monetary policy affects the general price level and not relative prices. As soon as inflation is brought under control market forces will operate in an effective and efficient way, so that relative prices will reflect the preferences and purchasing power of consumers on the one hand, and the production capacity of producers on the other hand. In fact, during a lasting process of inflation, not only the general price level increases but relative prices also are influenced in a heterogeneous manner and society may wish to counterbalance these influences on relative prices. Moreover, during the period in which the Friedman rule is applied, relative prices may in fact also change. There is then no logical necessity to embrace Friedman's idea that the economy can be left to private market forces if society does not like these changes.

With regard to economic policy, I prefer to distinguish between accepting Friedman's monetary proposals and the other parts of his theoretical approach. There are at least three reasons for this position. First, it would be of great help if a permanent incomes and price policy could be worked out which would bring inflation down in a direct way. Together with fiscal policy directed towards a more balanced budget than we are accustomed to today, this would enable monetary policy to be less severe and less tight, and therefore less harmful from the point of view of capital and labour destruction, and from that of the employment situation. Friedman and his colleagues have a case when they point out that an incomes and price policy has negative side effects on the workings of the labour market and of markets for capital and consumer goods, in that the allocation of resources may be disturbed. It seems to me, however, that, taking into account the heterogeneity of the different sectors of the economy as regards productivity and technical possibilities, it should be possible to influence the general levels of incomes and prices on the basis of global arrangements between unions and employers' organisations.

My second reason for making a distinction between monetarism in the narrow and the broad sense is that we cannot rely on market forces in view of the well-known failures of the market system: the market power of individual enterprises and other participants in the competitive struggle, the external effects of production and consumption, and the fact that public goods cannot for technical reasons be produced by the market system. We cannot afford to let industrial enterprises in The Netherlands, for example, pollute our soil merely because there is no market price on such bad behaviour. We cannot afford to allow nature to be allocated in the production process as a factor of production, while its preservation for present and future generations has a utility that cannot be expressed in terms of the market.

This brings me to my third and main reason why application of Friedman's rule is not sufficient to restructure our economy. In recent years we have seen that the market system is able to cope with quite a number of decision problems, for example, about the number of cars or bicycles that should be produced. But the market system is not able to deal with preferences for job satisfaction, for a friendly environment, for the preservation of nature, or with disutility for unemployment. These preferences cannot be expressed through the market mechanism.

This brings to the fore the significance of the formal and

subjective concept of welfare, a concept which refers to the level of satisfaction insofar as it depends on the allocation of scarce resources. In the coming years I think we shall experience what I call the operationalisation of this broad concept of welfare. New structures of decision making are needed within and outside the sphere of private enterprise. New institutional forms of decision making are needed in order to cope with new preferences for which the market mechanism is not an appropriate method of decision making. The market is not able to deal with these immaterial effects embraced by the broad concept of welfare; for this reason, Friedman's proposal that all policy measures be restricted to the application of his famous rule cannot be accepted.

It is my conviction that even in the coming months we shall see a recovery of the Dutch economy due to a lowering of the rate of inflation followed by a declining rate of interest, brought about by a strong monetarist approach to our economic problems. Even in England there is an improvement under way with respect to production and investment, particularly on a small-scale basis. It would be a major mistake, however, to think that the market economy will do the job on its own. The market can, as I have stressed, do a lot; it is a very efficient system for the allocation of resources if property rights are clearly delineated. In restructuring the public sector, authorities will doubtlessly make use of the positive properties of the market system. The market even has something to offer in the choice between different technological possibilities with uncertain and risky outcomes. Therefore, the market system is also useful from the point of view of stimulating innovation and creativity. But it cannot do everything. It cannot correct itself for its own failures. It cannot judge the pros and cons of new technologies from a social point of view. It is not able to produce the funds needed for the development of new technical possibilities which at first are very risky but which may nevertheless be worthwhile developing also from a social point of view. Above all, the market system is not able to ensure a distribution that will be accepted by all members of society. It is one thing to make more profits; it is quite another thing to allocate those profits in an acceptable way, especially in the direction of needs of an immaterial character.

Arnold Heertje

CONCLUSION

Monetarism – in the sense of application of Friedman's rule on the basis of the idea that too much money lowers its own value and therefore destroys our economic and political structure – has been and still is of enormous importance in our attempts to cure our economies, in that it forces us to balance preferences and possibilities in both the private and the public sector. For the future this implies that if we run across the same problems again, we may apply the same principles in order to recover once more. Monetarism, in the sense that an economy can be ruled only by applying Friedman's rule, does not take into account the drawbacks of the market as a system of decision making with respect to allocation, qualitative growth, and distribution.

In view of those who are already unemployed, and in particular the younger generation, it should be stressed yet again that our society cannot afford to rely only on the Friedman rule to stop the rise of unemployment, even if we are sure that in the long run the application will prove successful. It is our duty to care daily for those who are victims of the mistakes we have made together and to prepare even minor measures with which to improve their lot, so that a new perspective may be opened. While I consider monetarism in the restricted sense to be a blessing for mankind, its application in the broader sense would be a disaster, implying that we derive no lessons from the past: nothing could be more calamitous.

V

World Crisis and the Monetarist Answer

by ERNEST MANDEL

The world capitalist economy is in the midst of a grave international depression, a long depressive wave which started in the late 1960s and early 1970s, and which will certainly continue through the 1980s. There is sufficient statistical material available to indicate the gravity of the turn and to confirm the prediction which I made in the mid 1960s to the effect that, starting with the late 1960s, the rate of growth would decline to less than half what it had been [*Mandel, 1972*]. In actual fact, the decline has been even greater. In the EEC countries the rate of growth of national income declined from 4.6 per cent in the period 1953-73, to 1.3 per cent in the period 1973-81. Private real income, excluding government transfers, showed an even stronger decline, from around four per cent to about one per cent per year [*CEPR 1981*]. This has been accompanied by a very sharp increase in structural unemployment, which is the sharpest social expression of the long depressive wave. If we take at each high point of the successive recessions the official numbers of unemployed in OECD countries, we find that these have climbed from 10 million in 1971 to 18 million in 1975 to 28-30 million in 1982. The predictions are that, between 1981 and 1985, that figure might increase to 40 million. For the EEC alone, the Cambridge Department of Applied Economics predicts an increase in unemployment from nine million to 13.5 million, an increase of 50 per cent within the next four years [*Ibidem*]. These are government figures. In other words, they understate reality because they do not take into account all

79

those real unemployed that government statistics have eliminated from the labour market.

The most ominous aspect of these figures is that of youth unemployment. In countries such as the USA, France and Belgium, this is now in the neighbourhood of 20 per cent, if not 25 per cent, for school-leavers between 17 and 23 or 24 years of age. This means there are now several million young people in the Western countries who have never worked in their lives since leaving school, and who are also unlikely to find employment in the near future. British statistics indicate that in the third quarter of 1981, out of the labour force of 684,000 under 28 years old, 51 per cent were unemployed. The expected percentage for the third quarter of 1982 is 58 per cent and for the third quarter of 1983, 60 per cent (The *Observer*, 12 July 1981).

These figures only take into account the expression of long depressive waves in the industrialised countries. In most of the Third World countries, however, unemployment is even higher than the figures indicated here. With a few exceptions, particularly Mexico and some East Asian countries, the present recession has hit very hard indeed.

To give one example of a poor country: in Tanzania, export receipts do not cover any more than five per cent of the import bill. Foreign exchange reserves amount to import costs for no more than two or three days. Each week, factories have to close because of lack of raw materials or spare parts. Thousands of trucks and buses are immobilised for the same reason (*Le Monde*, 11-12 July 1982).

In the more developed Third World countries, the decline in industrial output in those supposed to be models of economic growth, such as Brazil or even South Korea for the year 1980, has been very great, amounting to five, six or seven per cent of manufacturing output, with all the consequences for unemployment, especially in those countries where social security institutions are non-existent, or at any rate far less real and effective than in the Western capitalist countries.

So far, the full weight of the depression has not yet been felt, at least not in the industrialised countries, due to the gigantic recycling of surplus capital, i.e. the continuation of a huge credit inflation. From that point of view, it has to be emphasised that the whole controversy about economic policy contains a large element of hypocrisy. People who shout that they favour the free market, and conservative and orthodox monetary policies, continue to fuel the economy with huge subsidies to bankrupt or semi-bankrupt enterprises. A very impressive list could be made of top multinational corporations which run huge annual losses but which continue to operate obviously with the help of bank credit and government subsidies: Chrysler, International Harvester, Massey Ferguson, AEG, Peugeot, Cockerill, Dome Petroleum, etc. This applies also to many nationalised corporations, especially in such countries as Britain and Italy. We hear a great deal about this, but much less about the bankrupt and semi-bankrupt private corporations. We hear much about bank credits to Third World countries and so-called socialist countries and much about their growing debts; but we hear less about the huge debts of industrialised countries such as Denmark, Belgium, Italy or France.

The general movement of huge debt and bank money expansion continues under the new conservative administrations in the West. This is undoubtedly a factor which has so far limited the depth of the depression; at the same time, however, it increases the threat of collapse of the bank system and the credit system. It is not accidental that President Reagan, of all people, came to the help of the Jaruzelski government in Poland when it was in danger of being declared insolvent; he was afraid this would cause a run on the banks as the result of the collapse of several large Western banks. He took over a guarantee of some of the debts of the Polish government. This is indicative of the fear that exists today in the highest circles, i.e. an important bank failure must be prevented because it could create an avalanche throughout the Western economy.

That is the general background, a very quick sketch to which many other factors could be added. The crisis is obviously not only an economic crisis. We are not only confronted with a depressive long wave of the capitalist economy, combined with periodic recessions. The present economic crisis has other aspects, such as an impasse in North-South relations of a social

81

and political nature, but I shall not go into that. It is against this background that one has to examine the function of monetarism which, in the first place, is not an academic theory at all.

Monetarism represents primarily a turn, and, if you want to use that word, a counter-revolution in the field of applied economics, of government policies: a counter-revolution inasmuch as it reflects a basic reversal of key values which were supposed to be at the bottom of government policies after World War II, or even after the big depression of 1929-32.

As a Marxist, I would add that behind this reversal of government priorities is a reversal of motives and priorities of the ruling class. The government priorities, of course, were well known, having long been platitudinous. The predominant trend of economic policies was linked to the doctrine of Lord Keynes. Full employment and the welfare state were supposed to be the main values of government policies throughout the West, and a profound political motivation was developed to justify this, especially in the Scandinavian countries and Britain where it was given its strongest expression. It was said that a high degree of social solidarity, of social integration and of political consensus, i.e. a greater probability of class collaboration, would be found only on the basis of decreasing social inequality and human misery, a gradual solution of the social question, through a qualitative advance of social welfare, of measures that would insure the average citizen against the consequences of economic fluctuations which are linked with a capitalist free market economy. This was seen as an axiom in the post-World War II period.

There were two aspects to this. First, it was embodied in official legislation, even in the USA where – it is easily forgotten – the Full Employment Act was actually adopted by Congress. Second, it was put into practice by policies of all governments, whether left or right, conservative or labour, leading in Britain to the famous formula of 'Butskell-ism', indicating that differences in that field between Labour and the Conservatives were really very small.

Today this consensus is completely broken. A total reversal of priorities has taken place. This started to develop in the late 1960s, with a growing ideological and even moral attack on the consequences of welfare statism, and gained momentum with

82

the arrival in power of conservative administrations such as that of Mrs Thatcher in Britain and President Reagan in the United States, which base themselves partly or largely on monetarist theories.

This reversal is very clear. The main priority is to struggle against inflation rather than to achieve full employment. If it is necessary to sacrifice full employment for a successful fight against inflation, then that must be done. If it is necessary to sacrifice government expenditure in the social field in order to reduce state expenditure and state budget deficits, then that must be done. If it is necessary to reduce real wages in order to bring about greater monetary stability, then this also must be done. This reversal of priorities can be linked with a change in priorities of the ruling class. This is not purely academic and it is certainly not platonic. Keynesianism, gradual reformism, the building-up of greater social consensus, known in France as *concertation sociale* – these were policies which came in reaction to the great depression of 1929-1932/33 and to threats against civil liberties and parliamentary democracy which were seen as its results in the 1930s. Such policies were applied within the context of a long wave of economic growth in which they were practical, and could be applied with a measure of success. Many doctrinaire Keynesians or neo-Keynesians are of the opinion that the 1950s and 1960s represented the most progressive and prosperous period in the whole history of the Western world. Whatever price had to be paid by Third World countries and whatever the imbalances on a world scale, there is some empirical evidence to confirm that opinion, at least, for many privileged Western countries.

The reversal, again, was not accidental. It came after a long period which, according to Marxist analysis of the long-term laws of motion of the capitalist mode of production, led to a long-term decline in profitability. This decline was not caused basically by high wages, but was certainly difficult to reverse with a working class that had been made powerful by long-term full employment, increased unionisation, increased militancy, and increased expectations after such a long period of economic growth. Under these circumstances, the main motivation for the bourgeois class was to create conditions in which this crisis of profitability could be reversed. This reversal of motives was

83

not a product of the slump, but a product of the boom. The drama for the monetarists and the bourgeoisie is that the application of the new policies coincided with the slump, and, as a consequence, all the results of the slump became amplified beyond expectations.

Whereas moderate monetarists thought it would be sufficient to have a mild measure of unemployment in order to change the social and economic atmosphere, they were faced with a situation of more than three million unemployed in Britain. When you already have massive unemployment as a result of market forces, the result of the reversal of economic and monetary credit policies adds secondary forces to amplify unemployment.

Here I must take exception to the thesis of some of my Keynesian friends whom I prefer, of course, to the monetarists, because it is naturally nicer to take money from the rich and give it to the poor than to take money from the poor and give it to the rich. But this does not mean that, in my opinion, the Keynesians are right. They say that monetarist policies have caused the present depression, but I see no evidence of that. They have amplified the depression, have made it grave and more difficult to overcome, but they have not caused it. That cannot be proven, chronologically or empirically. The depression started before the application of monetarist policies. Its causes are easy to specify, if you take the main sectors of the world economy. The roots of those causes go deeper than those of monetarist policies.

To put it even more strongly: there is an organic link between the motivating forces of the long postwar boom and the way in which it has reversed itself into a long-term slump. Because of the deep structural crisis of world capitalism, the depression of the 1930s could only be overcome through war and permanent inflation. The capitalist world economy floated towards prosperity on a sea of debts: debt inflation, credit inflation, bank money inflation, were endemic to the boom. This boom, it is true, was supported by the supremacy of American imperialism, which was correlated to the supremacy of the dollar, underlining the Bretton Woods monetary system. But debt inflation in the USA sooner or later had to lead to the inconvertibility of the dollar and to the collapse of the Bretton

Woods system, which in turn accelerated all those forces that were leading up to the slump.

The trouble with my Keynesian friends is that, by making Mrs Thatcher and Mr Reagan, to say nothing about Milton Friedman, the main culprits, they let the capitalist system off the hook. I would prefer to make the capitalist system the main culprit, and to see Milton Friedman and the others as mere secondary actors in the drama. The basic laws of the motion of capitalism have caused this crisis of over-production, which is, after all, the 21st crisis in the 150 year-old history of the world market for industrial goods. It is difficult to see these minor actors, who have only popped up on the world stage in the last few years, as the principal cause of an historical movement which has been going on for 150 years, and which will continue to do so as long as the system exists. I take exception, therefore, to making the monetarists responsible for more than their due.

Conservative politicians and their monetarist inspirators merely repeat on a smaller scale in some countries and on a larger scale in others, policies which were experimented with as long ago as the early 1930s during the previous long-term slump, policies which will lead to the same result as that to which deflation led in the old days.

Before we discuss that any further, there is an ideological and moral dimension to this whole problem which should first be examined. Behind the application of monetarist policies there is a reversal of government priorities, i.e. a reversal of priorities of the bourgeois class, of the ruling class. It is not easy to bring about such a reversal and it should not be seen as a conspiracy. It should not be thought that a group of people come together to find ways and means by which to persecute the working class, and then set about changing people's minds in order to achieve that goal. That is not how history comes about. The objective operation of the international capitalist economy has imposed upon national governments the need to react against balance-of-payments crises caused by higher-than-average rates of inflation, insofar as these governments lack either the social interest or the political will to break out of that framework. Such reaction leads to deflation by measures against which a properly unionised working class would revolt. It therefore becomes necessary to create a social and political climate in which the unions lose their strength to paralyse government's deflationary policies. Hence the idea that a bit of unemployment will weaken union power. Hence the abandonment of the target of full employment.

There is a whole series of mediations, some of an academic and scientific nature, some of a pragmatic, practical origin, others which are more clearly ideological. I want to stay a moment with this last category because it is the least acknowledged in countries such as The Netherlands or Belgium or the Scandinavian countries, being even less operative there than in the United States, Britain or France, for example.

It is not easy to modify prevailing ideology because ideas have the habit of lingering on even after they become useless for those who invented them. Those who consume the ideas take them seriously, assimilate and maintain them even though their use for their producers has ceased. This struggle of what might be called 'the new right', the 'silent majority' or the 'moral majority', has been a difficult and uphill struggle against values which its own class had created in an earlier period, values which are still deeply-rooted in large parts not only of the middle classes and the intelligentsia, but particularly of the working class. Even for the ruling class and its ideologues, however, this reversal of priorities from formal social solidarity to egoism thinly disguised as individualism, is accompanied by an element of bad conscience which is difficult to avoid.

John Kenneth Galbraith, with whom I do not always agree, has coined a beautiful formula on what the monetarists try to convince the public about [*Galbraith, 1981*]. According to Galbraith, the monetarists want to restore the Puritan work ethic. In order to explain that the loss of the Puritan work ethic is at the root of the present crisis, however, you also have to explain that there is a crisis because people work too little. It seems rather bizarre to posit that, when more than 30 million people are out of work through no fault of their own, the crisis is caused by the fact that people do not work enough. Let us forget that paradox for a minute, however, and let us admit that people really work too little. Why do they work too little? In the logic of the Puritan work ethic, the rich work too little because taxes are too high, because they lack incentives, because it is not worth their while to work more, i.e. because they are too poor. The poor work too little because they get too much money from the state, i.e. because they are too rich. So what is the solution? If the rich are too poor and the poor are too rich, the solution is obviously that you take money away from the poor and give it to the rich. If the rich become richer they will work more. And if the poor become poorer they will also work more. That is the basic message of monetarist policies.

It is not easy, of course, especially with the Puritan ethic, to swallow such a message (it is better not to use the word 'science' in that context). A whole ideological underpinning therefore has to be created in order to justify a policy with new values. That is what the 'new right' is all about.

Some of these new values are not new at all; indeed, they go back to much earlier times than poor Lord Keynes who today is so denigrated. They upgrade things that were common ruling class ideology 60, 80, or 100 years ago, not just in the 1950s. To the social Darwinists of yesterday and the socio-biologists of today, men and women are *not* created equal; they are created unequal. It is of little use to have equal educational standards, because the origins of inequality are biological and genetical. It is of little use to redistribute income, whether nationally or internationally, because it will not create more equality or justice. It will only work against economic growth. Besides, there are already too many people, and if a few less live it will be all the better for the rest, and so on and so forth. Some of these reactionary theories set the clock back a century or so. Even Bismarck knew better, and he died in 1898.[1]

These attempts at ideological counter-revolution have political implications which are rather ominous. In Western Europe and in the United States, there was a first phase of what might be called the disorientation of people who were faced with a sudden end of the welfare state and of full employment. This affected the working class in particular, since the trade union movement's leadership had not educated the members to face mass-scale unemployment and to react against it. Moreover, the first wave of unemployment hit the weakest parts of the working class, i.e. the immigrant workers, the women, the youth. It had somewhat less effect on the stronger battalions of the working class, who were much better insured and defended. This is now changing, however. In this present recession, contrary to that of 1974-75, the really big bastions are being hit. I am referring to the attacks on Fiat in Italy, British Leyland in Britain, Lorraine and Walloon Steel in France and Belgium, AEG in Germany. When this is accompanied by the first reductions in social welfare payments, a second wave of working class reaction starts, as it has already started in Belgium, Italy, Portugal and other countries.[2]

There is thus a very big risk for the bourgeoisie with the reversal of policy priorities. When they take the axe to the basis of social accord, i.e. of class collaboration and reformism, they might well get a lot of social strife in reply – social strife under a social and political relationship of forces, both national and international, which will be far less favourable to the bourgeoisie than in the 1930s, and with a working class that is much more numerous and an international set-up which is much more shaky. Under these circumstances, the real risk that the bourgeoisie is running is what I would call the French risk. It can even be put in the form of a formula: mass unemployment and massive attacks against social security, plus universal franchise and political freedom equals the risk of huge electoral victories, landslide victories of the left.

In the last French legislative and presidential elections, the two left-wing parties, the Communist Party and the Socialist Party, together received over 55 per cent of the popular vote, and they now occupy 65 per cent of the seats in parliament. This has never happened before in the history of Western Europe. I would say it is possible (of course, not automatic or unavoidable, but possible) that in the long run, if you keep all the elements of the equation, i.e. mass unemployment, massive attacks against social security plus universal franchise and full-scale political freedom for the working class, the 'French risk' for the bourgeoisie could be repeated in many other countries.

The temptation for those who take seriously the restoration of profitability as the key priority of economic policy, or, as we could perhaps call them, the consistent monetarists, will be to take away some part of this equation. The first part which could be taken away is full-scale political freedom. The second part is universal franchise. As regards the attack on unemployment and social security, there is no chance that they will make any concession.

By 1985, under the Reagan Administration's budget and tax policy, the *positive* impact of federal budget and tax policy on households with more than $48,000 in annual income will be around 140 billion dollars; on households with annual incomes of $11,500, the net effect will be *minus* 24 billion dollars. The proposed 1983 budget, for instance, would cut programmes for the poor such as child nutrition, Medicaid and welfare by 10 to 18 per cent.[3]

It is difficult to see how, under those circumstances, the bourgeoisie could still retain its moral self-assurance by claiming ingenuously with George Gilder [*1981*], that love and altruism are the true essence of capitalism.

This is therefore the political danger behind this ideological counter-revolution, which flows from the counter-revolution in the field of economic and social government policies. There is again a causal, structural relationship between the surge of irrationality in the field of the social sciences and of political ideologies, and such possible attacks against political democracy. Once you are convinced that people are *not* equal, why should you allow them equal formal political rights? Once you try to convince everyone that there are biological elites who have the right to be rich at the expense of others, and have the right to rule, why put them in a position where they can be pushed out of government by the votes of those who are of a lower order, who are biologically of inferior quality, and who should have no say in the way in which the government and the state are run?

There is an ominous inter-relationship between some of the more irrational theories of the lunatic fringe of the extreme right and some of the extreme conservative convictions which are already defended not only by the lunatic fringe,[4] but also by strongly entrenched political conservative fractions and some of the official mouthpieces of conservative economic policies. In certain Third World countries, in fact, this interrelationship has already been demonstrated in practice. I am thinking in the first place of our unfortunate contemporaries in Chile, but that correlation could come to Europe as well, via such countries as

Turkey, Portugal or Spain. It is not difficult to imagine under what circumstances, and with what results. What I am talking about, once again, is thus not platonic or academic.[5]

Finally, let us examine some of the reasons why, from an economic point of view, the monetarist answer to the crisis cannot be a success. I state once again, in order not to be misunderstood, that I am not a Keynesian, I am a Marxist, and orthodox Marxists see economic crisis at one and the same time as crisis of *over-production of capital*, and as crisis of *over-production of commodities*. This is how Marx himself described it.

Marxists have a *dual* and not a *mono*-causal explanation of the crisis. They say that crises occur at one and the same time because there is a crisis of profitability and too little purchasing power to buy the accumulated mountain of commodities. If you only solve one side of the problem you do not solve the crisis. That is what is wrong with both Keynesians and monetarists: they make a divided attack on a united phenomenon.

The Keynesians attack the demand side, which is not wrong, of course. If you have unsold commodities and you distribute more demand, more purchasing power, especially to the poor who do not save, some of the excess commodities will be sold, and some of the excess productive capacity will be put to use again. That is elementary. Those who deny it, deny common-sense logic. But the monetarists are also right when they say that given the crisis of profitability, you will not have an upsurge of investment if profitability remains low or falls even lower as a result of the distribution of more money to the workers and to the poor. That is also obvious. There is a recorded historical failure of all Keynesian attempts to overcome a grave crisis of over-production with the aid of pure demand-increasing, reflationary government measures. They can succeed in the initial phase, as the Mitterrand government has succeeded, in mildly increasing sales and output and employment in the consumer goods sectors. But they cannot trigger off a cumulative wave of economic growth through a wave of increased investment, which they hope will come after the wave of increased sales and output of consumer goods. That does not follow automatically, as we have seen during the New Deal in the United States and as we shall see soon in Mitterrand's France.

But the other side of the story is also true. The monetarist reasoning has very grave theoretical weaknesses[6] and there is already sufficient evidence that it will fail. Here the reasoning goes the other way around: if profitability goes up, investment goes up, employment goes up, and growth goes up. There are several glaring gaps in this mechanical scenario. First of all, even though profitability goes up, productive investment does *not* automatically go up as well. That needs a whole series of preconditions because capitalists can use their increased profits for other purposes than investment, at least investment in job-creating productive sectors. They can hoard, they can export their capital to other countries, they can speculate. In the second place, an increase in productive investment does not automatically increase employment. That depends on the nature of technology and on the whole economic context. If the economic context is one in which the prime motivation of firms is to reduce labour costs, there will be tremendous pressure in favour of what we can call rationalisation investments, which suppress more jobs than they create. This is all the more so, as we are in the midst of a third technological revolution, which is not yet over by far; according to certain experts, in fact, it has hardly started. This technological revolution, linked to semi-conductors, micro-electronics and so on and so forth, is job suppressing, not only in the manufacturing sector but also in the so-called service or tertiary sector, which was the big reserve for job creation during the expansive long wave which we experienced in the 1950s and 1960s. There is no doubt, in my opinion, that all government policies aimed at saving money in public administration, in the health service, in education, and all attempts to rationalise distribution and financial institutions, which are in the throes of a crisis, go in the direction of application of micro-electronic techniques in all those areas which were the big fields of job expansion during the previous 25 years, and which will now be placed under the sign of job suppression.

There is thus no reason to assume that there is any mechanical correlation between redistribution of income in favour of higher incomes and of profits on the one hand, and an

91

increase in investment, employment, output and general social well-being, on the other hand. All the evidence leans the other way. For a long period to come, such policies will increase unemployment, increase social tension, increase human misery, without having any of the beneficial effects on growth and employment which some of their proponents hope for.

There is another side to this story which should be stressed and that is the economic consequences of deflationary policies in the medium and the long term. If we look at the long-term effects of social expenditure, we know very well that there is a productive result of what we could call social and material infrastructural expenditure. To spend money on education, on health, on roads, on bridges, on all forms of material and social infrastructure, is not to waste money from a macro-economic point of view, as some pseudo-liberal economists still light-heartedly believe. It is another form of investing, without *immediate* productive results, it is true, but with growing productive results that will be reaped after five, ten or fifteen years. Development economists and politically-aware people of the Third World know that very well. It is one of the strongest cases for development policies to say that if you spend more money on education now, if you build better ports now, you are not wasting money. Even if this does not lead immediately to an increase in material production, it certainly does so in the medium and long term.

What is true for the Third World, however, is also true for the industrialised countries. If you spend less on education, on health, on infrastructure, if you let the roads decline, bridges break down, then even in a country such as the USA you will reduce the national income in the next 10 or 15 years. If your transport system breaks down, if it takes longer for goods to reach the customer, you will have to spend more on transportation costs; the costs will become higher and the overall productivity of the economy will decline, and that is a waste.[7] That is a grave consequence of the application now of deflationary policies, which will be felt after a certain time. In the USA even conservative municipal administrations are up in arms today against the Reagan Administration which has brought them to near bankruptcy. Many municipalities are quite unable to spend even the minimum amount which they need to spend, not in order to expand the infrastructure but to keep it at its present level, making no allowance at all for population growth and the need to incorporate technical progress. These consequences will be felt at a later stage, but when the history of the second half of the twentieth century is written, they will be seen as an indictment of monetarist deflationarists and conservatives just as strongly as the indictment that is made today against the Keynesians for fuelling inflation.

The end result, the consequence of which is most ominous and grave, is that there is one field of economic endeavour in which no one in the ruling circles seriously talks about economising, about the need to apply caution and the need to reduce expenditure, i.e. the field of military expenditure. And it is no accident that, as in the 1930s, the graver the crisis becomes, the stronger the social tension created by conservative policies becomes; the more the whole economic and social context seems to be laden with insoluble contradictions, the greater the temptation becomes to have recourse to violence, violence on a national scale and violence on an international scale which means war, in order to solve these contradictions.

If today we have a universal austerity attack against the working class and the conquests of the labouring population in the field of social security, this austerity offensive is linked more and more with a re-militarisation offensive, an offensive which puts at the centre of politics the increase of military expenditure, the build-up of weapons systems that become more and more destructive, and more and more risky for the survival of the human race.[8] We have lived through such a combination before and we know the consequences. I do not think that a 'solution' of the present world crisis at the price of a third world war, which would be a nuclear world war, is in any way a reasonable perspective. Therefore, I think that we have to take the political and social consequences of this monetarist counter-revolution extremely seriously; that we have to consider it as a major challenge for the future, not only of political democracy but for the very survival of the human race.

NOTES

1. Michael Billip [*1980*] has shown convincingly the interrelationship between the upsurge of a new racism in contemporary psychology and the development of far-right-wing political trends. The correlation between the rise of mysticism, obscurantism, occultism, etc. in the 1920s and the pre-Fascist ideological climate is too obvious to dismiss the ominous implications of similar trends today.

2. A study by the OECD [*1981*] draws attention to the grave political and social consequences which could arise out of the appearance of huge deficits of the social security institutions and the ensuing cuts in social security benefits.

3. *New York Review of Books*, 29 April 1981.

4. The French author Pierre Krebs [*1981*], influential in the so-called Thule Seminar which operates on a European-wide scale, has systematised many of these ideas. The French ideologue Alain de Benoist, who belongs to the same circle, and had links with the Giscard d'Estaing administration, does not hesitate to write: 'It would be unjust [*sic*] if all human beings had a soul; it is just that only a few succeed in finally achieving their self-creation, to give themselves a soul. Only whoever is master of himself can give himself a soul' (quoted in *Die Zeit*, 14 May 1982).

5. Ideologues such as Milton Friedman who, in the face of more than 200 years' evidence to the contrary – from Bonapartism to Fascism to the Chilean dictatorship – still continue to claim that only capitalism can guarantee free thought, free press and free individuals, should at least ponder how their 'moral majority' allies in the Reagan Administration are already busily organising library censorship in at least 20 per cent of schools in the USA, banning even books like *The Diary of Anne Frank* or Aldous Huxley's *Brave New World*. The freedom of the individual *does* seem to collide with the needs to defend the social system. A more general contradiction is that between the assertion of that freedom and the proclaimed need to accept alleged 'objective economic laws' (including laws of 'technological progress'). Again, capitalism is on weak grounds if it asserts a moral superiority on the basis of liberal ideas, which reality tramples on day after day. It has to find other, less liberal, 'moral' justifications for its reactionary policies.

6. Many authors have drawn attention to a basic weakness: the impossibility to give a precise definition of the quantity of money, and to determine *simultaneously* the quantity and the velocity of circulation of money.

7. *Business Week* (26 October 1981) has published a dossier on the municipal crisis in the USA. The reduction of current infrastructural expenditure has caused such decay that maintenance costs alone will rise to 660 billion dollars over the next 15 years.

8. Again, the monetarists provide an ideological under-pinning for this switch in government expenditure priorities, by coolly asserting that national defence is a 'true' public good, while education is a good which 'could be private' and public monopoly of subsidised education should perhaps be ended in the interest of 'more efficient schools' [*US Government 1982*].

REFERENCES

Benoist, A. de., 1982, in *Die Zeit*, 14 May.
Billip, M., 1980, *Psychology, Racism and Fascism*, Birmingham.
Cambridge Economic Policy Review, 1981, Vol. 7, No. 2, 'The European Community: Problems and Prospects'.
Galbraith, J. K., 1981, 'Up from Monetarism and other Wishful Thinking' in *New York Review of Books*, 13 August, pp. 27, 30-32.
Gilder, G., 1981, *Wealth and Poverty*, New York, Basic Books.
Krebs, P., 1981, *Das unvergängliche Erbe-Alternative zum Prinzip der Gleichheit*, Tubingen, Graberet-Verlag.
Mandel, E., 1961, 'L'Apogée du néo-capitalisme et ses lendemains', *Temps Modernes*, No. 219-20, August-September.
Mandel, E., 1972, 'The Permanent Arms Economy and Late Capitalism', Chapter 9 in *Late Capitalism*, London, New Left Books.
OECD, 1981, 'L'état protecteur en Crise', Paris.
US Government, 1982, *Economic Report of the President*, Washington, US Government Printing Office.

VI
Monetarism and the State Socialist World

by MICHAEL ELLMAN

MONETARY THEORY AND POLICY IN THE STATE SOCIALIST WORLD

The essential feature of monetary *theory* under state socialism is the stress that is laid on the importance of a cautious monetary policy in maintaining a stable price level. The Banking School type view maintains that money creation should reflect, and be determined by, the volume of real economic transactions. The Currency School type view maintains that excess money creation is possible and harmful.[1] Money created in excess of the real need for money is regarded as inflationary, a disorganising and thoroughly undesirable feature of economic life. It is inflationary, since an excess supply of money in the hands of the population causes suppressed inflation in the state supply of consumer goods and services, and open inflation in the private supply of goods and services (e.g. free markets for agricultural products). It is disorganising, since inflation can have adverse effects on the labour supply to the state sector (with the planned allocation of labour being disturbed by shortages and queues, black markets and unplanned income differentials) and on national economic planning. Planning the whole economy must inevitably be largely in price or value units, for reasons of aggregation. This becomes very difficult if absolute and relative prices are continually changing. Excess money is undesirable, since shortages and queues, black markets and speculation, are

96

demoralising and undermine popular support for socialism, and have an adverse effect on income distribution (with real income being redistributed to those with political power, or strong economic position, such as retail trade employees, grandmas, or connections) [*Griffith-Jones, 1981*].

The essential feature of monetary *policy* under state socialism is the wide variety of instruments that are used to try to ensure that the cautious monetary policy dictated by theory is in fact implemented [*Garvy, 1977*]. These instruments include:

(a) wage fund planning,
(b) the state budget,
(c) the balance of money income and expenditures of the population,
(d) the credit plan of the state bank, and
(e) the role of the state bank in controlling and supervising plan implementation.

The basic instrument of monetary planning under state socialism is wage fund planning. This is a variety of incomes policy that operates by control over the wage bill of each enterprise or association. In this it differs from incomes policy under capitalism which normally seeks to control the incomes of particular categories of employees. (Not owning the means of production, the state under capitalism is unable to give orders to individual firms as to their maximum permissible wage bill.) Wages are the main source of money in a socialist economy, and wage fund planning can be a very effective means of monetary control.

As under capitalism, the state budget in socialist economies plays a key role in balancing the availability of resources and claims on resources. The published state budget normally shows a surplus. In the socialist countries deficit financing is regarded with a fierce aversion that would bring the whole-hearted support of the most conservative Western bankers and financiers. The purpose of running a budget surplus is to prevent demand pull inflation. Some official data are set out in Table 1, which shows clearly that, with the exception of Hungary, the published budgets of the CMEA countries normally

Michael Ellman

TABLE 1

Incomes and Expenditures of the State Budget in the CMEA (billions of national currency)

	1960	1970	1975	1976	1978	1980
Bulgaria						
Income	2.4	5.7	9.3	9.2	10.6	13.3
Expenditure	2.3	5.6	9.2	9.0	10.5	13.2
Surplus	0.1	0.1	0.1	0.2	0.1	0.1
Hungary						
Income	72.7	171.9	313.3	320.4	382.9	423.0
Expenditure	73.8	175.7	316.2	322.9	386.4	427.5
Deficit	1.1	3.8	2.9	2.5	3.5	4.5
DDR						
Income	49.8	70.6	114.7	117.6	132.6	160.7
Expenditure	49.5	70.0	114.2	117.1	132.1	160.3
Surplus	0.3	0.6	0.5	0.5	0.5	0.4
Cuba						
Income	n.a.	n.a.	n.a.	n.a.	9.7	9.4
Expenditure	n.a.	n.a.	n.a.	n.a.	8.8	9.6
Surplus	n.a.	n.a.	n.a.	n.a.	0.9	(0.2)
Mongolia						
Income	1.1	2.0	2.8	3.2	3.4	4.1
Expenditure	1.0	1.9	2.7	3.0	3.3	4.0
Surplus	0.1	0.1	0.1	0.2	0.1	0.1
Poland						
Income	209.5	389.6	720.1	881.4	1103.5	1215.2
Expenditure	200.1	379.3	701.7	799.5	994.2	1246.3
Surplus	9.4	10.3	18.4	81.9	109.3	(31.1)
Romania						
Income	58.2	133.3	238.6	254.5	300.8	298.0
Expenditure	55.4	130.9	236.2	250.1	299.3	296.8
Surplus	2.8	2.4	2.4	4.4	1.5	1.2
USSR						
Income	77.1	156.7	218.8	232.2	265.8	302.7
Expenditure	73.1	154.6	214.5	226.7	260.2	294.6
Surplus	4.0	2.1	4.3	5.5	5.6	8.1
Czechoslovakia						
Income	109.9	105.9	278.1	292.2	286.3	306.3
Expenditure	107.1	194.3	273.8	290.1	283.9	304.2
Surplus	2.8	11.6	4.3	2.1	2.4	2.1

Source: Statisticheskii ezhegodnik stran-chlenov Soveta Ekonomicheskoi vzaimopomoshchi 1981 [Moscow, 1981], 59.

show a surplus and that the occasional deficit (for example, Poland and Cuba in 1980) indicates a crisis.

The balance of money incomes and expenditures is an important planning instrument. It shows on the one hand the incomes of the population and on the other hand their expenditures, and is used to try and equilibrate the two.[2]

The credit plan is a plan for the credit extended by the state bank. It corresponds, *mutatis mutandis*, to the global credit ceilings sometimes imposed by West European Central Banks or the wider monetary targets of central banks in other countries pursuing monetarist policies. The purpose of the credit plan is twofold. First, to ensure that bank credit is allocated in accordance with the national economic plan. Secondly, to prevent bank credit generating demand pull inflation.

The state bank plays a major role in checking and controlling plan fulfilment. All economic organisations keep their accounts with the state bank which can check whether funds are applied in accordance with the plan. Whereas private banks in capitalist countries often facilitate frustration of the goals of the state, in socialist countries the state bank is one of the agencies (others are the central statistical office, the control commission, and the Communist Party) striving to ensure plan fulfilment.

It would be a mistake to conclude from the above that monetary policy under state socialism is problem free. This is certainly not the case. For example, wage fund planning is a well-known cause of inefficiency and waste, and is unable to prevent wage drift. It encourages inefficiency and waste since in effect it provides enterprises with an incentive for overmanning. If they were to reduce their labour force their wage fund would be reduced correspondingly and they would gain no benefit. Indeed they would probably lose, since some bonuses and pay levels depend on the size of the wage fund and the number of employees. That it is unable to prevent wage drift has been shown by McAuley [*1979: 250*].

Furthermore, although the published budgets of CMEA member countries normally show surpluses, it is unclear whether or not this is a true reflection of the actual situation. According to Birman, the true USSR budget actually shows a significant and growing deficit, with important inflationary results [*Birman, 1981*].

Michael Ellman

RELATIONSHIP OF ABOVE TO MONETARISM

Before considering the relationship of monetary theory and policy in the state socialist world to monetarism it is necessary to consider what is meant by 'monetarism'. Some may be tempted to say that monetarism is known by its works, but that is possibly a little harsh. It is clear, however, that a precise definition is very difficult, since there is no single monetarist model. For the purposes of this discussion, monetarism will be taken as a body of thought stressing the importance of the aggregate stock of money in macroeconomic relations, especially those determining quantities denominated in money terms, such as national income.

It is clear that there are a number of important similarities between state socialist doctrines and monetarism. First, both agree that money is a veil, i.e. that the monetary and real sides of the economy are essentially separate. Hence, both agree that monetary policy should concern itself with the price level and the real economy be regulated by other policies.

Second, both focus on stocks. The monetarists focus on the stock of money, central planners on stocks of goods.

Third, both advocate the insulation of domestic money supply from the world economy. The monetarists advocate doing this by floating the currency. In this way they hope to ensure that fluctuations in the world economy only affect the exchange rate, while stable prices are maintained by stable non-inflationary growth in the domestic stock of money. In the state socialist countries it is done by the system of price equalisation subsidies which reimburse the losses or capture the profits of international trade resulting from the differences between the domestic and world price levels.

Fourth, both agree about crowding out. That is, both agree that private and state expenditures are competitive, and that an increase in state expenditure causes a reduction in private expenditures. In fact, under state socialism there is a phenomenon that Portes has termed 'super crowding out'.[3] Under state socialism, an increase in state expenditure can cause a *greater* decrease in private expenditure. It can do this because not only are state and private expenditures direct competitors for resources, but an increase in state expenditures leading to a greater degree than normal of (open or suppressed) inflation may have adverse effects on the labour supply or the marketed output of agriculture.

Fifth, both agree that a major aspect of fiscal policy is to facilitate monetary policy. Under capitalism, monetarists argue that fiscal policy should not be aimed at influencing the level of economic activity but at a low borrowing requirement so as to restrain monetary growth. Under socialism, economists argue that the budget should always be in surplus so as to help the struggle against inflation.

Sixth, both oppose an expansionary macroeconomic reaction to oil price shocks. Keynesians regard huge oil price increases as deflationary for oil importers, and advocate dealing with them by expansionary macro measures so as to preserve full employment. Monetarists, on the other hand, regard a change in relative prices as a normal phenomenon and an increase in the money supply to deal with it as inflationary and undesirable. Discretionary policy is inevitably destabilising, whereas steady growth of the money supply provides the stable framework in which the economy can adapt to the change in relative prices [*Fischer, 1980*]. Marxist Leninists support the monetarists in this matter and regard an expansionary response by an energy importing country to oil price increases as absurd. The oil importing country has lost part of its national income as a result of an adverse movement in the term of trade, a socialist planner would reason. Therefore, the domestic utilisation of resources (for consumption, investment or defence) must be reduced if inflation is to be avoided.

Seventh, both regard the activities of independent trade unions as economically undesirable. Monetarists, of course, reject as a complete illusion the Keynesian idea that trade unions can cause inflation. (According to monetarism, only central banks can cause inflation.) Monetarists regard trade unions as undesirable since they cause unemployment, particularly in socially vulnerable marginal groups (blacks, the young, women, the elderly). By organising labour market monopolies and driving wages above market clearing levels, big labour strengthens its position at the expense of causing terrible social problems. Similarly, central planners regard independent trade

101

unions as incompatible with socialist planning. By interfering with matters that should be left to the discretion of the planners they introduce chaos and anarchy into economic life.

Although there are some important points of agreement between monetarism and Marxism-Leninism, there are also important differences. These concern in particular, *emphasis*, the *monetary equation*, and *implementation*.

For a monetarist, monetary policy is of great importance since it can prevent inflation and provide a stable framework in which real forces can determine the real variables (for example, employment and growth). For a central planner, on the other hand, monetary policy is a relatively minor aspect of economic policy. The real aspects of the economy, for example, technical progress, the structure of production, changes in the labour force or the location of production, or raising consumption; and the control system – the management system – are much more important.

The traditional monetary equation $MV = PT$ can be given four interpretations: weak monetarist, strong monetarist, Keynesian and central planning.

According to the weak monetarist interpretation, V (the velocity of circulation) is a constant. Hence, the equation asserts that changes in M (the quantity of money) are the principal cause of changes in PT (the money national income), subject to long and variable lags.

According to strong monetarism, V is a constant and in addition T is determined exogenously (by the real economic forces). Hence, changes in M determine P. Inflation is determined by the rate of change of the money supply.

For a Keynesian, P (not T) is determined exogenously (by the level of money wages). Assuming that V is a constant, the monetary equation now implies that changes in M determine T, or as the Keynesians say, that the national income is determined by the level of demand.

For a central planner, both T and P are determined exogenously (by the planner). Assuming that V is a constant, the monetary equation implies that M is determined by PT. This is the kernel of a theory of non-inflationary monetary policy in a planned economy, in which the planned level of national income determines the desirable, non-inflationary, level of the money stock which should be aimed at. Looked at another way, it is the kernel of a theory of repressed inflation in centrally planned economies (when the non-inflationary level of the money stock is exceeded).

As far as implementation is concerned, for a monetarist monetary policy is primarily a policy to be implemented by a central bank. It is the central bank which must pursue a steady growth in the M chosen for control. It is the 'Fed' that was responsible for the Great Depression. For a central planner, monetary policy is primarily a policy to be implemented by wage fund planning. It was Gierek's failure to control wages, according to this view, which generated the Polish internal disequilibrium of the 1970s, and Kania's failure to control them which led to a dramatic deterioration of the internal market situation in 1980/81. For a monetarist, incomes policy is extremely undesirable because of the inefficiencies it causes. For a central planner, incomes policy is an indispensable part of a planned economy and the main method for ensuring control over the money supply.

WHY IS MONETARISM FEASIBLE AND PROGRESSIVE UNDER STATE SOCIALISM?

The basic reason why monetarism is feasible under state socialism is that the financial sector is much simpler. There is essentially only one bank, the state bank, and there are virtually only two kinds of financial asset, namely, cash and deposits in the state savings bank. Therefore, one does not have all the problems, about which M to control, M1, M2, M3, etc. ... Nor does one have the problem of private banks which are seeking to expand their loans regardless of official monetary policy. In addition, the economy is not one which is coordinated through the market, but one in which the planners have replaced the market by planning as the main coordinating factor.

It is these institutional differences which explain why it is that the factors which are central in Keynesian theory and on which the Keynesian theory of money and banking are based, simply have no applicability under socialist conditions. If you look either at Keynes himself, or to a sympathetic contemporary interpreter such as Minsky [*1975*] or Davidson [*1978*], one

103

finds an extensive discussion, for example, of the role of the banks. A lot of attention is devoted to how, over the cycle, the banks can accelerate the upswing and destabilise the economy in a downswing by precipitating deflation. This kind of analysis is interesting and important for market economies but simply incompatible with the institution of state socialism, where it is the planners and not the bankers who are in charge. Similarly, there is a sophisticated – and for market economies very relevant – Keynesian discussion about money as the link between an irrevocable past and an uncertain future. That also has no application for state socialist countries. There, in principle at any rate and in some cases in practice as well, it is the plans and the planners who are the link between past and future.

Because of these institutional differences, the simplicity of the financial system and the non-existence of private banks and a wide variety of financial assets, monetary policy is quite feasible under state socialism. Given that monetary policy is feasible under state socialism, is it progressive?

Following Kalecki, it has become conventional to argue that the fundamental technical difference between capitalist and state socialist economies is that the former are demand constrained and the latter supply constrained. In a supply constrained economy, increasing demand will not increase output. Instead, it will just disorganise the economy, increasing shortages and possibly reducing labour inputs into the socialist economy and the sale of agricultural output to the state, and possibly reducing marketed agricultural output as a whole. Hence, Keynesian or populist policies would be only harmful.

This distinction between supply constrained and demand constrained economies has very important implications. Take the question of unemployment. Strict monetary policy under conditions of socialist planning is not (normally) associated with the creation of unemployment. It could not be because the socialist economies are supply constrained economies, where all resources are permanently in short supply. Strict monetary policies and full employment, under these conditions, are perfectly compatible.

The above argument is sometimes challenged on two grounds. First, it is often said, there *are* unutilised resources in socialist countries, for instance, 'on the job unemployment'.

Although this is correct, this kind of unutilised resource cannot be mobilised by increased demand. Its mobilisation requires structural changes ('economic reform'). Secondly, it is sometimes suggested that in a country such as China or Vietnam, cautious monetary policy is associated with open unemployment. This is undoubtedly correct. It is, of course, also correct that the cancellation of investment projects financed by foreign loans reduced a potential source of inflationary pressure and reduced the chance that at some future date inability to service loans would lead to a Polish-style crisis. Furthermore, it is in general correct to assert that under state socialist conditions the regressive effects on income distribution often associated with monetarism under capitalism, do not exist. There is no redistribution towards wealth holders and the banks and against the newly unemployed.

In evaluating socialist monetarism it should be borne in mind that, as mentioned above, for socialist monetarism as for capitalist monetarism, independent trade unions are a great nuisance.

THE IMPACT OF WESTERN MONETARISM ON THE STATE SOCIALIST COUNTRIES

The impact of Western monetarism on the socialist countries has been felt in two ways. First, in the *interest rates* on their foreign debts. Second, in their *budgetary policy*.

The switch from Keynesianism to monetarism as the theoretical basis of Western monetary policy has led to international interest rates reaching very high levels. This has had a dramatic adverse effect on those socialist countries which are heavy debtors. The worst affected country is Poland. The Polish crisis looked at from an economic point of view is basically just a balance of payments crisis of the sort that I, as a Briton, am only too familiar with, and the sort that many Third World countries have experienced. It is a balance of payments crisis largely arising, not from current trade deficits, but from the burden of debt servicing. (In 1981, Poland's hard currency debt service ratio was 115 per cent [*Ellman & Simatupang, 1982*].) For the CMEA in general, and for Poland and Romania in particular, the current high level of international interest rates – a direct result of the domination of monetarist ideas in economic policy making – is a tremendous burden.

An interesting result of this, is that monetarism in the West has strengthened CMEA integration. CMEA integration is something on which, for obvious reasons, the USSR is very keen. Despite this influential backing, CMEA integration faltered in the 1970s because for many CMEA members the expansion of trade with the West was more attractive than the expansion of trade with their CMEA partners. Since a number of CMEA countries are now virtually bankrupt, their credit-worthiness on the euromarkets has evaporated, and they have experienced enormous difficulties in expanding their hard currency exports and balancing their hard currency balance of payments, CMEA integration has received fresh support. Poland, formerly critical of Soviet ideas on CMEA integration, is now very dependent on the USSR for supplies, markets and political support. Polish opposition to Soviet ideas about CMEA integration has, accordingly, evaporated. This is an example of how Reaganism is strengthening the position of the USSR.

The development of monetarism and the eclipse of Keynesianism in the West, has had a certain influence on budgetary policy in the socialist countries, particularly in China.[4] Traditionally, China, like other socialist countries, has had a surplus in the published budget. In 1979 and 1980, however, it had significant deficits. A discussion took place on how to respond to this. Some people argued that there was no need to worry: 'the great economist Keynes has shown that deficits can be quite a good thing. Many Western countries have deficits, these are the countries we want to learn from and catch up with, so perhaps we should learn some economics too, and have a big deficit, so as to stimulate the economy.' The counterview, however, was also argued strongly: 'budget deficits may be desirable under capitalist conditions. Under socialist conditions, however, the Keynesian policy of stimulating the economy by budget deficits is inappropriate.' It is not an accident that Milton Friedman was invited to China to lecture on economic policy, and it is not an accident that the Chinese took drastic measures in 1980 and 1981 to bring their state budget back into balance. They regard that as necessary, and they have been strengthened in that conviction by the arguments of monetarist economists and the high professional evaluation which they have received in the Western world.

SOVIET ANALYSIS OF THE 'MONETARIST CONTROVERSY'

There is a considerable Soviet literature analysing 'the monetarist controversy'.[5] The views expressed therein can be summarised in the following six theses.

First, the duration and depth of the controversy, its heated and embittered nature, reflects the depth of the crisis in the capitalist world.

Second, both schools of thought are wrong. The Keynesians are thought to be wrong, of course, because they exaggerate the possibility of government regulation achieving full employment and steady growth. For Marxist-Leninists, naturally, that is a complete illusion. The monetarists are thought to be wrong since they exaggerate the extent to which unregulated capitalism can achieve social goals. For Marxist-Leninists, to suppose that any kind of capitalism, regulated or unregulated, can achieve social goals, is a profound illusion.

Third, as far as monetary policy under capitalism is concerned, Soviet authors argue that it is difficult to implement and its effects uncertain. In this respect they endorse part of the Keynesian critique.

Fourth, as far as the causes of inflation are concerned, Soviet authors argue that it is a complex process, in which political factors, especially the role of the state in attempting to overcome the contradictions of capitalism, are central. The weakness of the monetarist analysis of inflation, it is argued, is that it is purely superficial, ignoring the structural factors. For example, the contribution of private ownership of the means of production, the struggle of the workers for improving their living standard and more generally the class struggle in its totality, the role of the state and the degree of monopoly.

Fifth, Soviet writers argue that monetary expansion is a powerful factor not only in propagating inflation but also in causing it.

Sixth, Marxist-Leninists consider that monetarism as a body

107

of thought is simply a bourgeois ideology which attempts to transfer blame from where it really belongs, namely, the capitalist system as a whole and the monopolies and their price forming policies, and persuade people that all problems are a result of faulty government policy.

If one reads the American literature about Soviet monetary discussion and Soviet economic theory in general, one gets the impression that Soviet writings are rather childish and not worth paying attention to. In my view, however, at any rate in this case, the Soviet analysis is quite sophisticated and largely correct.

CONCLUSIONS

My conclusions are as follows:

1. The rational kernel of monetarism is politically and socially neutral. It is not, for example, necessarily associated with typically conservative, or as they are now often called, supply-side views. It can be associated with a wide variety of political and institutional arrangements. (By 'rational kernel of monetarism' I mean the ideas that money matters, that the supply of money can be controlled, and that it is important to do so.)

2. The rational kernel of monetarism (just like the rational kernel of marginalism) is quite correct.

3. Socialist monetarism is entirely rational. It is not true that policy makers in the state socialist countries do not understand monetary policy or that they pay too much attention to Milton Friedman, or that they have sold out to the capitalists. On the contrary, under the institutions which they have, their tight monetary policy is entirely rational.

4. One can learn a great deal about economic theory and economic policy in market economies from the study of state socialist countries.

5. What is wrong with monetarism is that it is concerned essentially with planning only one small sector of the economy, namely money, and not with planning the rest of the economy as well.

6. It is precisely under socialist conditions that one has the best

opportunities for, and the least problems with, monetary policy.

7. The duration and depth of the monetarist controversy that took place in the West in recent years anticipated and reflected the actual economic crisis through which we are living. In this controversy, both schools are essentially wrong.

NOTES

1. The reference is to a well-known controversy about monetary and banking policy in early nineteenth century England. See Schumpeter [*1954: 725-31*] or Podolski [*1973: 12-18*].

2. *Metodicheskie ukazaniya k sostavleniyu gosudarstvennogo plana razvitiya narodnogo khozyaistva SSSR* [*Moscow, 1969: 524-46*].

3. Portes [*1981*]. I have borrowed heavily from this paper for my contribution to this book.

4. *Beijing Review*, 13 April 1981, 21-22.

5. See Usoskin, [*1976*].

REFERENCES

Birman, I., 1981, *Secret Incomes of the Soviet State Budget*, The Hague, Martinus Nijhoff.

Davidson, P., 1978, *Money and the Real World*, London, Wiley, 2nd ed.

Ellman, M., & B. Simatupang, 1982, 'De economische crisis in Polen' (The Economic Crisis in Poland), *Economisch Statistische Berichten*, 23 June.

Fischer, S., ed., 1980, *Rational Expectations and Economic Policy*, Chicago, University of Chicago Press.

Garvy, G., 1977, *Money, Financial Flows and Credit in the Soviet Union*, Cambridge, Mass., Ballinger.

Griffith Jones, S., 1981, *The Role of Finance in the Transition to Socialism*, London, Allanheld.

McAuley, A., 1979, *Economic Welfare in the Soviet Union; Poverty, Living Standards and Inequality*, London, Allen & Unwin.

Minsky, H. P., 1975, *John Maynard Keynes*, New York, Columbia University Press.

Podolski, T. M., 1973, *Socialist Banking and Monetary Control: The Experience of Poland*, Cambridge, Cambridge University Press.

Portes, R., 1981, *Central Planning and Monetarism: Fellow Travellers?*, Cambridge, Mass., NBER Working Paper.

Schumpeter, J., 1954, *A History of Economic Analysis*, London, George Allen.

Usoskin, V. M., 1976, *Teorii deneg*, Moscow.

109

VII

Structuralism vs Monetarism in Latin America: A Reappraisal of a Great Debate, with Lessons for Europe in the 1980s

by DUDLEY SEERS

THE LATIN AMERICAN DEBATE

Those of us who have worked in Latin America regard with some astonishment the economists of Western Europe and North America. Locked in a debate about the merits of monetarism, these economists are apparently in total ignorance (judging from the books, journal articles and lecture courses on inflation which now abound) of a controversy which has been going on for a quarter of a century in Latin America. Even more astonishingly, they seem to know little or nothing about the results of attempts there to apply monetarist policies – or of neglecting financial constraints. I shall argue that if our profession had done their homework they would have found important clues for solving some of our own problems in the 1980s.[1]

Latin America in the late 1950s and early 1960s was the site of the first great monetarist/structuralist debate. A number of countries had developed what was then considered scandalously fast rates of inflation. Table 1 shows the price experience of a number of countries in the 1950s, after the short-term economic effects of World War II had died away. This was the background to the debate. There were some semi-industrialised

I am grateful for comments from Ricardo Carciofi, Stephany Griffith-Jones, Karel Jansen, Philip O'Brien, Hubert Schmitz, John Sheehan and John Wells.

110

TABLE 1

Average Increases in Retail Prices, 1945/51 to 1958/60
(per cent per annum)

Countries with rapid inflation

Chile	38
Argentina	26
Brazil	20

Countries with moderate inflation

Peru	8
Mexico	8
Colombia	7

Countries with slow inflation

El Salvador	3
Ecuador	1
Venezuela	1

Source: ECLA [*1961*].

countries with chronically rapid inflation; some with moderate inflation, at a lower stage of industrialisation; and some chronically dependent on primary exports with rates of inflation no greater than could be accounted for by trends in the world economy.[2] (El Salvador's experience was similar to that of all countries in Central America, with the partial exception of Guatemala.) The battlelines formed between those in the IMF, reflecting professional opinions in the industrial countries, who argued that deflationary policies were essential, and those who took the view that inflation was a lesser evil than stagnation for a country with serious social problems, and that some degree of inflation was inevitable if these problems were to be tackled.

The monetarists had (and have) a simple prescription for avoiding inflation: keep the rate of increase in the money supply to no more than is needed for the growth of output. But the real issue, of course, was (and is) the validity not so much of monetarism as of the parent doctrine from which it sprang – neo-classicism, Chicago style, which is really a prescription for a highly capitalist development strategy. If factor and product markets are allowed to function smoothly without price distortions (for example, by exchange controls, due to monopolistic factors or government intervention) resources will allocate themselves in a way that maximises growth. Since profit margins will be relatively attractive in an economy short of capital, funds will pour in from outside. Should prices show a chronic tendency to rise, and the currency become overvalued, foreign 'confidence' may be lost and so the money supply must be severely restrained, which means limiting government spending and wage increases.

This advice has been dispensed by missions sent by the IMF from the 1950s onwards, when their financial help was sought to deal with chronic balance of payments deficits in Latin America. In effect, their counsel was to combat inflation by opening the economies to international influences and to the discipline these imposed, even if it meant postponing economic development.

This was not a welcome message to political leaders, especially those in Argentina, Brazil and Chile, who were – for whatever reasons – trying to industrialise in a hurry, and to finance educational schemes and capital works which would lay the basis for future development; it was especially unwelcome to those who also wanted to become less dependent on foreign countries for markets and capital.

'Structuralism' provided them with a rational critique of monetarism. It took various forms in the hands of different writers, but a common assumption was the overriding importance of fast economic growth, because of the pace of population increase and rising expectations.

Industrialisation was seen by the Latin American structuralists, especially Raúl Prebisch, as an essential element in economic growth, in particular in the larger economies, already semi-industrialised and partially urbanised. He had argued, since the late 1940s, that shortage of foreign exchange tended to block growth in countries which relied on exports of primary products. This line of argument had been supported by the Prebisch/Singer 'terms of trade thesis', that the terms of trade tended to deteriorate in countries exporting primary products. This led to a basic contrast between the 'centre' (called by other writers the 'core') of industrial countries and the 'periphery', the primary product exporters.

Protected import substitution was thus needed – a theme popular with the growing urban populations of all classes. In due course it would ease the foreign exchange constraint, and enable the countries of Latin America (and I believe Prebisch always had Argentina especially in mind) to join the centre (and treat the USA as an equal).[3]

Prebisch was Executive Secretary of the Economic Commission for Latin America at the time. Other economists there such as Anibal Pinto, Osvaldo Sunkel and myself brought out its implications for analysing inflation.

A basic theoretical criticism raised by structuralists was that monetarists were too aggregative: one had to look at particular sectors to understand inflationary pressures, not just at the character of finance ministers. Fast growth led by the manufacturing sector implied inevitably some price rises. Markets did not function as well as neo-classicists assumed. Supply 'bottlenecks' appeared because of structural rigidities. (The same critique applied to another aggregative school, the Keynesians.)

Import substitution in manufactures required the recruitment of factory workers with the necessary skills, who often had to be recruited far afield, and anyway the wages that had to be paid were high by local standards. Protected products were naturally more expensive than the imports they displaced (otherwise protection would not be necessary). In fact, they were often produced by monopolies or oligopolies, with sub-optimal production runs, due to the small size of national markets. (This was one of the theoretical justifications for the Latin American integration schemes in the 1960s, in which Raúl Prebisch also had a hand.)

Agriculture was one obvious supply bottleneck. Food consumption had risen faster than the population, but in most countries of Latin America much of the arable land was in very large holdings and the owners, often absentees, appeared keener to emulate quasi-feudal lifestyles and/or to treat land as a source of capital gains than to maximise income. Infrastructure was also inadequate. Transportation facilities were meagre and had been constructed to take primary products to the ports.

113

Electric power capacity was inadequate for the modernisation of productive sectors and the growth of consumption.

Basic tendencies to price inflation were 'propagated' by rises in incomes of all the social groups that were sufficiently well organised to safeguard themselves from the effects of price increases, for example by linking their incomes to consumer prices.

But if price rises were an inevitable accompaniment of fast industrialisation, they could not be inhibited entirely unless this was abandoned. Even then, the relief would only be temporary, since structural bottlenecks would remain and prices would rise again as soon as industrial growth was resumed. Some inflation had to be tolerated, at least temporarily. The only fundamental cure for it was a high level of investment in sectors that were lagging and this was hardly compatible with monetary restriction.

There were three particular implications of the structuralist approach. First, it required planning (called 'programming' in the publications of ECLA, perhaps out of deference to US sensitivities). The government could not leave the development of key sectors such as electric power to the play of market forces. It had to forecast future needs and provide for them. ECLA documents showed how to do this, with detailed country programmes, the main output of the Commission in the late 1950s.

Second, foreign aid was necessary to bridge the 'gap' in the balance of payments which was an inevitable, though believed temporary, consequence of programmes of rapid industrialisation.

Third, although Prebisch himself did not, at that stage, have much to say about the concentration of income,[4] other authors in the structuralist tradition put more emphasis on it, not merely as something socially obnoxious but as an obstacle to carrying out development programmes. The main proponent of the 'stagnation thesis', Celso Furtado, saw it as a major obstacle to growth. In the case of Brazil, such a low proportion of national income was in the hands of the general public that mass markets for locally produced manufactures could not emerge, and industrialisation would be blocked. Hence rises in the income shares of wage-earners and peasants were essential.

POLICY EXPERIENCES

The history of Latin America has, unsurprisingly, hardly settled the debate. Both structuralism and monetarism have been somewhat undermined by research and by subsequent events, but also both in part justified.

Structuralist Programmes

The 'stagnation thesis' is now quite dead, killed by the Brazilian boom. The explanation is not that inequality has been reduced there; on the contrary, and in this respect even the crude estimates of income distribution may not be misleading [*Fishlow, 1972*]. Part of the explanation is that the patterns of the lower income groups' spending have shifted from food to manufactures [*Wells, 1977*], a shift that can be noted in other countries too [*Filgueira, 1981*].

TABLE 2

World Production and Trade Indices 1957-59
(1913 = 100)

Production	– Manufactures	381
	– Primary Products	203
Volumes of trade	– Manufactures	251
	– Primary Products	182
Unit Values in Trade	– Manufactures	259
	– Primary Products	257

Source: Maizels [*1971, 80*].

Moreover, the 'terms of trade thesis' has not survived long-term research. A great deal depends on what period one takes – and even more on what primary commodities one is talking about: the experience of beverage crops has been very different from that of metals (let alone oil).[5] Any trends are gradual in relation to fluctuations. The thesis would have had a firmer

115

quantitative basis, as Table 2 shows, if it had referred to *volumes* of trade: exports of manufactures definitely tend to grow more rapidly, reflecting higher income elasticities.

However, these theses are not essential to structuralism. More telling has been policy experience. The protected industrialisation advocated by the structuralists ran into serious difficulties. In the first place, it did not bring the expected easing of the demand for foreign exchange. Although import coefficients fell, the absolute volume of imports continued to rise. Indeed, much of the imported technology was highly capital-intensive and energy-intensive, leading to heavy dependence on imported equipment and oil. The industries concerned often needed imported intermediate products and services. Moreover, the concentration of resources on industry has made many Latin American countries food importers. Finally, since in some countries industrialisation has been largely carried out by foreign capital, it has led to a big increase in profit remittances (partly concealed by transfer pricing).[6]

Protection not merely encouraged monopolistic tendencies, it was so heavy as to weaken the normal ceilings on wages, leading to increases greatly exceeding those in productivity. Exports of manufactures were further damaged by overvalued exchange rates (permitted in order to check the consequential pace of inflation).

In the second place, the experience of populist governments – Quadros in Brazil in the early 1960s, Allende in Chile in the early 1970s, the first phase of the Peronist return in Argentina in the middle of the 1970s – demonstrated the dangers of reacting so strongly against monetarism as to spurn fiscal restraints,[7] and adopting general (rather than selective) policies of expansion at a pace far outstripping the possible response of the productive sectors.

Chile provides the clearest illustration. One cites it with reluctance because to do so seems to excuse the intervention of the military leadership in alliance with the CIA. These certainly carry a grave responsibility for the killings in the coup and subsequently. But any objective analysis must also give some weight to the economic policies of the *Unidad Popular* government. And unless the lessons of the Chilean experience are drawn, it will surely be repeated there – and elsewhere.

116

In retrospect, the election manifesto may well have doomed the government before it ever took office. This promised big increases in health and educational services, a large training and infrastructure programme, reduced rents and mortgage payments, higher wages and higher pensions, abolition of sales taxes and no more 'scandalous' devaluations.[8]

The government did in fact try to carry out this combination of policies. Soon after taking office, wages were raised by nearly 70 per cent, twice the increase in consumer prices in the previous year, more for those with families. The wage increase also meant a sharp jump in public expenditures, which were further increased by the government fulfilling commitments to expand social services.

Not surprisingly, imports were stimulated and exports inhibited – perhaps with more effect than was achieved by the US embargo on copper sales. Aid agencies such as the World Bank reduced their support and the controls adopted to check the foreign exchange outflow simply led to a flourishing black market. Moreover, since the Allende government lacked a majority in Congress, it could not finance its rising outlays by increases in taxes, which in fact fell, so that a very big budget deficit appeared. This could not be covered (as in Europe) by recourse to the capital market (which is virtually non-existent), so a 'flexible' monetary policy was followed and money supply doubled in its first year, at the end of which the escudo was at last devalued.

This highly expansionist policy was advocated by the government's theoreticians, such as Pedro Vuskovic, on the grounds that spare capacity clearly existed in industry: but there was a limit to the capacity that could in practice be easily mobilised, especially since the nationalisation of a number of companies (sometimes without due legal process), together with increased worker participation, naturally meant a degree of disorganisation, at least temporarily. This limit was reached after about a year during which the economy did in fact spurt forward. Then scarcities developed. Although the election manifesto promised an end to inflation, the moderate price rises inherited from the Frei regime started to accelerate and, by mid-1973, food shortages were serious and prices were rising by something like 50 per cent a month. Since the mass base of government was limited (illustrated by the fact that it never achieved an overall majority in any national election), conditions were created in which a coup was feasible.[9]

As Stephany Griffith-Jones [*1981*] has pointed out, in an analysis of events of Chile (and also of the early experiences of Communist governments in Russia and Czechoslovakia), it is precisely those governments that attempt radical transformations which most need a cautious monetary policy. Yet it is very difficult for them even to realise this need, still less implement it. They will have become accustomed to opposing the monetarist policies of previous regimes, and glaringly obvious needs for social expenditures will be pressed by their constituency. While what is recommended by the IMF is often largely what they need to do anyway, the fact that it is proposed by an outside agency is fatal to its chance of acceptance.

As a result of economic and political crises, import substitution policies have been abandoned throughout much of Latin America. 'Planning' – which was always largely window-dressing – has given way to laissez-faire. For administrative and political reasons, state intervention proved ineffective if not damaging.

The Monetarist Counter-Offensive

On the face of it, the Chicago economists seemed by the end of the 1970s to have won the day. In several countries, the military dictatorships that had overthrown the populist governments held real wages down and achieved fast economic growth, helped by rising exports of manufactures, a welcome diversification.

There are major flaws in this picture, however, even from a strictly economic viewpoint.[10] The governments of Brazil and Chile in particular have only been able to maintain their expansion, still largely oil-intensive, by very heavy inflows of capital. Not much of this has taken the form of foreign direct investment, the level of which has been disappointing, suggesting that industrialists overseas are not, after all, convinced of the practical reliability of the Chicago model.[11] What these governments have attracted has been overwhelmingly *loan* capital, so debts have soared. The foreign exchange problem has not been abolished, simply postponed. Since their trade balances are still in deficit and they now have to borrow merely to service existing debt, growth strategies of this type are already proving unsustainable.

The spurts in growth have in fact petered out (though in Brazil, where Chicago theories were in practice considerably tempered by the nationalist ambitions of the armed forces, the boom lasted for over a decade). Yet inflation has by no means come to an end. Indeed, in Brazil prices are doubling every year (and have in fact risen about a hundredfold since a series of military governments committed – periodically – to stabilisation started in the mid-1960s). In Argentina the pace became even faster in 1981 when the government gave up the attempt to maintain an overvalued exchange rate.

These developments support fairly clearly the structuralist proposition that in countries with such defective markets, financial policy would have to be so restrictive if it were to eliminate inflation entirely as to be socially and politically intolerable. Even modified Chicago doctrines can only be imposed in some countries by military dictatorships.

The experience of the dictatorship in Chile, where the Chicago influence is strongest (and tariffs were reduced to 10 per cent with very few exceptions), appears more comforting to the monetarists. The rate of inflation seemed to have been virtually eliminated. But this was really the only positive achievement. It was partly due to an increasingly overvalued exchange rate, which could not be sustained indefinitely, any more than it was in Argentina. Here the 'gold standard' variant of monetarism has been dominant under which foreign exchange equilibrium will be achieved by falling relative prices of domestic products. (By contrast, the Brazilian model was based on the belief that the exchange rate, too, should reflect market forces.) But the payments deficit has been mounting rapidly in Chile as well and reached more than three billion dollars in 1981. More has to be borrowed even to service the enormous debts that have been incurred.

Moreover, the cost has been very heavy in terms of reduced social services, and unemployment has risen to over 15 per cent – or 20 per cent if one allows for the makework scheme 'empleo minimo'. In the past year the economy has been rocked by many major bankruptcies; and the government has taken over several banks and insurance companies because of administrative irregularities. Capital investment has remained low by historical standards (less than 15 per cent of GDP, much of which went in fact to finance inventories of imported consumer goods), and import penetration has destroyed (as in Argentina) much industrial capacity. The per capita national income appears to be only about 10 per cent higher than it was a decade ago [*CEPAL, 1982*].

Propagandists for these regimes argue that they have been unlucky in their timing. Those of Argentina and Chile, in particular, came to power when the world economy was losing dynamism. Prices of commodities such as copper have weakened, yet import prices, especially of oil, have soared, and loans have become very expensive in the main capital markets.

But this does not seem very convincing. Those adopting economic policies based on opening-up the economy can hardly blame their failures on adverse developments in the rest of the world – just as it was rather unbecoming for Latin American Marxists to express shock at the ferocity of the reaction their policies induced in imperialist governments.[12] In each case a model was adopted without, apparently, appreciation of its obvious implications.

THE LESSONS FOR LATIN AMERICA

In retrospect, what has really been at issue has not been whether to adopt monetarism, or other neo-classical policies of the Chicago type, but what position Latin American governments should adopt vis-à-vis a world economic system which, without being doctrinaire, one can call neo-colonial. This system allows the corporations of the neo-colonial powers to invest in Latin America with little fear of expropriation, to import materials and fuel from them, and to sell their goods in Latin American markets.

The populist governments mentioned above were in effect trying to extricate themselves partially (in the case of Chile almost completely) from the system. But the system has been very beneficial to many (perhaps most) political interests in the neo-colonial powers. What the history of this period shows is that they can block attempts to secede from the system, by the use of political influence, military force and financial pressures (including the withdrawal of aid), singly or in combination. They are moreover helped by some powerful groups in the countries concerned.

When we describe structuralist programmes as implying secession from the neo-colonial system, we see what a task is involved. To tackle it needs not only a good resource base but also strong and united internal support, excellent administrative capacity and leadership, including strict financial policies. One might add that help from an external power, in practice the Soviet Union, would also be necessary. The governments concerned did not have these sources of strength: in particular the Soviet Union has not been able to take on any more clients after Cuba.[13]

Chicago neo-classicism is in effect a policy of unconditional integration into the system. It involves a loss of sovereignty and, as we have seen, social costs, especially when the machine is not performing well. One major lesson of Latin American experience which applies outside the region too, is that while ideologies like those of Chicago or the Marxists or the structuralists (or their later incarnation as dependency theorists) may be useful simplifications of reality, especially for pedagogical purposes, and may yield some emotional satisfaction, they are dangerously misleading as guides to policy. Politicians in any country who, on the base of a vulgar version of one ideology, say that if they are elected they will guarantee to 'eliminate inflation' or 'reduce unemployment' are seriously misleading the public, because these depend on external and internal forces over which they have very little influence.

THE LESSONS FOR EUROPE

The Latin American policy controversies of past decades seem particularly relevant today in Western Europe. At the time of the Great Debate, the Latin American governments mostly concerned (Argentina, Brazil and Chile) were attempting rapid development to contain social pressures and to move from dependent status to acceptance as major industrial countries –

hardly yet a possibility for most other Third World countries. The problem for West European governments is to develop sufficiently quickly to retain their place in the vanguard.

The monetarist case is virtually the same (except for less emphasis on the significance of the exchange rate). Its inflexible application, whatever the period and country, constitutes indeed its major weakness. In Europe, too, this is aggravating economic problems and the characteristic association between economic liberalism and political repression can be discerned in embryo. Much industrial capacity is being destroyed (not all of which is obsolete), and new investment is low.

There is a vicious circle: declines in employment lead to increases in unemployment benefits which cause governments to cut other forms of spending, thus further reducing employment. The 'automatic stabiliser' of Keynesian theory is thus not allowed to operate.

This raises the question: what would the Keynesians do? The exact form of their critique and the precise policy recommendations vary of course; there are almost as many Keynesian schools as Keynesians! But their central policy advice is to focus on the level of demand rather than the money supply or the 'public sector borrowing requirement'. Since there is much spare capacity, demand can be safely increased even if this means a big monetary expansion too.

This approach is both economistic and aggregative, like the monetarist; a structuralist critique of monetarism might be more appropriate in Western Europe also (and for that matter Eastern as well).[14]

What this would mean can only be indicated in outline here; even Latin American structuralism is more an *approach* (with a list of agenda items) than a *theory*. But clearly its application would start here too with imperatives for *structural* change. These do not lie, as in Latin America, in the dire poverty of the majority of the population or the high birth rate or the excessive dependence on exports of primary products. In Europe the needs are different: to reduce unemployment and to maintain levels of living. These imperatives imply first changing the structure of industry so that its products can compete effectively with the manufactures of Japan, the United States, South Korea, etc., and secondly, reducing oil-intensive consumption so that there is less reliance on imports (in the British case, so that more oil is available to export).

There would be fairly general agreement on this. The question is how such structural changes are to be made. As in Latin America, they appear too big and too urgent to be achieved by market forces alone. There are obstacles to adjustment here too, but they are also different. Land tenure is far less important, for example. In Western Europe, trade union practices, housing subsidies, out-of-date educational systems, are major hindrances to the mobility of labour, and labour shortages (local to an industry or a region) co-exist with unemployment. Rates of interest, strongly influenced by those in the United States, inhibit the necessary capital investments.

There also seem to have been declines in industriousness, educational ambition and entrepreneurial drive. Such changes in attitude are virtually impossible to measure, and though this enables the typical economist to ignore them, especially if they are ideologically inconvenient, it does not make them a whit less important. Anyway, such developments would hardly be surprising in view of the general achievement of fairly comfortable levels of living. They are evidenced indirectly by the slowing of productivity growth in the 1970s, especially in Britain, and by the fact that few of the unemployed apply for the menial jobs which are available (which are thus largely done by migrant workers). The one possible justification for monetarist policies is that they may have helped dispel such inertia.[15]

But if responsiveness to stimuli has been blunted in at least some of these ways, aggregate Keynesian models are unhelpful. Reserves of industrial capacity could turn out to be misleading here too. Global reflation by Keynesian macroeconomic policies would, as in Latin America, soon run up against a combination of shortages of particular types of labour, physical bottlenecks and balance-of-payments difficulties, reflecting in particular the world oil shortage, which is still latent even if temporarily (and marginally) unimportant. Moreover, the trade unions would certainly take advantage of reflation to 'propagate', if not initiate, price rises. The result would be an acceleration of inflation: the scale would scarcely be comparable with that experienced in Chile or Argentina in the 1970s, nor would the outcome be the same, but it could still be too

123

politically embarrassing to be sustained. France may in due course provide an illustration.

The fundamental cure to inflation seems to lie rather in carefully chosen priorities (as in Japan) for industrial development to fit a European development strategy, the precise detail and mix of measures varying from country to country, together with policies to reduce dependence on imports and on external markets. In other words, to withdraw partially from the neo-colonial system. But continental, not national withdrawal. A combined policy of industrial protection and expansion would be much safer in a unit as large as the European Community, complemented by strategies in other sectors, especially energy. Then development could be resumed without inflation.

NOTES

1. For a picture of the Latin American debate two decades ago, see Baer & Kerstenetsky [*1964*].

2. If we took the 1970s, we would find that countries fall into the same three groups, though one would have to multiply the inflation rates by three to over ten.

3. For a detailed presentation of Prebisch's arguments see Prebisch [*1962*].

4. He now justifies this (in a symposium, as yet unpublished) as being attributable to the remnants of his neo-classical education. I wonder, however, whether it was not due rather to the, doubtless subconscious, wish to keep property-owners part of the nationalist alliance whose needs he was articulating.

5. See Spraos [*1980*]. It is true that some countries show a deterioration (especially if the period covers the past decade), but the net effect over the decades is relatively very small. Bosworth & Lawrence review recent research relevant to the thesis, though without mentioning Prebisch (or Singer), and conclude that even when fuel prices are excluded 'the relative prices of primary commodities during the 1975-79 period is almost identical to that of a century earlier.' [*1982: 37*].

6. Realisation of these costs of import substitution was a major factor in converting in the 1960s many Latin American structuralists into dependence theorists.

7. In Seers [*1981*] I argue as in the past, for an eclectic approach that gives some role to financial policy in achieving development without severe inflation.

8. This manifesto is reprinted in Zammit & Palma, IDS [*1973*].

9. A former Secretary to the Ministerial Economic Committee, Sergio Ramos, is of the view that:

> Given its political orientation and its Programme, the UP Government had no choice but to apply an economic policy which would satisfy the short- and long-term necessities and aspirations of the people. The resultant economic evolution, and in particular the inflationary process, were generated not by the policy's application, as seemed to be the case, but by the insufficient revolutionary transformation of Chile's economic and social system. [*1979: 353*].

If this is the conclusion generally drawn by former leaders in that government, its next period in office may well be even shorter than the last one.

10. See David Felix: 'Latin American Monetarism in Crisis' and other articles in *IDS Bulletin*, 1981, Vol. 13, No. 1 (*Monetarism and the Third World*).

11. A few years ago I was at a meeting in Havana between Castro and some US businessmen, where Castro played on this apprehension. He said that if he were in their place, considering investment in Brazil or Cuba, he'd be apprehensive about possible social revolution in the former, whereas in Cuba 'ya occurrió!'

12. A particularly naïve example of this was the protestation of the Allende government at the suspension by the US Export-Import Bank in July 1971 of credit facilities (to buy Boeing aircraft). As the cover to S. Sideri, ed. [*1979*] says: 'The UP underestimated the degree to which international capitalism would see the UP policies as a threat and would react accordingly.'

13. Following the Cuban revolution, the Castro government, despite major blunders in the 1960s (especially in financial policy), managed to withstand US (and internal) pressures – though it was helped not only by massive Soviet support but also by wavering and ineffectual US policy.

14. This would help demolish the paternalistic belief that development studies is concerned with poor countries in the tropics. It might also help to discourage the naïve transfer of European neo-classical doctrines (whether monetarist, Keynesian or Marxist) to other continents.

15. The economic policies of the present British government may well, indeed, be the best possible ones in the circumstances. They have discredited doctrinaire monetarism, but have achieved some very necessary shifts in attitudes that are likely to last!

REFERENCES

Baer, W, & I. Kerstenetsky, eds, 1964, *Inflation and Growth in Latin America*, Homewood, Ill., R. D. Irvin.

Bosworth, B.P. & R. Z. Lawrence, 1982, *Commodity Prices and the New Inflation*, Washington, Brookings Institution.

CEPAL, 1982, 'Notas sobre la economia y el desarrollo de America Latina', No. 335/6.

ECLA, 1961, *Inflation and Growth*, Santiago, unpublished.

Felix, D., 1981, 'Latin American Monetarism in Crisis', *IDS Bulletin*, Vol. 13, No. 1, *Monetarism and the Third World*, 6-13.

Filgueira, C., 1981, 'Consumption in the New Latin American Models', *CEPAL Review*, Vol. 15, 71-110.

Fishlow, A., 1972, 'Brazilian Size Distribution of Income', *Papers and Proceedings, American Economic Review*, Vol. 62, 391-402.

Griffith-Jones, S., 1981, *The Role of Finance in the Transition to Socialism*, London, Frances Pinter.

Maizels, A., 1971, *Industrial Growth and World Trade*, Cambridge, Cambridge University Press.

Prebisch, R., 1962, 'The Economic Development of Latin America and its Principal Problems', *Economic Bulletin for Latin America*, Vol. III, No. 1, 1-22.

Ramos, S., 1979, 'Inflation in Chile and the Political Economy of the *Unidad Popular* Government', in Sideri, ed., 1979, 313-62.

Seers, D., 1981, 'Inflation: the Latin American Experience', *IDS Discussion Paper No. 168*, Institute of Development Studies, Sussex.

Sideri, S., ed., 1979, *Chile 1970-73: Economic Development and its International Setting*, The Hague, Martinus Nijhoff for the Institute of Social Studies.

Spraos, J., 1980, 'The Statistical Debate on the Net Barter Terms of Trade Between Primary Commodities and Manufactures', *Economic Journal*, 90, March, 107-28.

Wells, J., 1977, 'The Diffusion of Durables in Brazil and its Implications for Recent Controversy Concerning Brazilian Development', *Cambridge Journal of Economics*, Vol. I, 3, 259-79.

Zammit, A., & G. Palma, eds, 1973, *The Chilean Road to Socialism*, Sussex, IDS.

VIII
The IMF Prescription for Structural Adjustment in Tanzania: A Comment
by BRIAN VAN ARKADIE

INTRODUCTION

This paper relates to the approach which the IMF has favoured in dealing with the current Tanzanian economic crisis. As such, it concentrates on issues as they emerge in the Tanzanian case and does not attempt to address the more global issues raised by the role of the IMF in the current economic crisis, except to note two preliminary points.

Any examination of a particular IMF programme will appropriately concentrate on the implication of the package for the country in question. However, the IMF, operating internationally, is attempting to solve global problems; indeed, its national prescriptions reflect a view regarding the management of the current world economic crisis. Given the Bretton Woods intent to avoid a repetition of the 1930s, it must be an increasing irony that the IMF apparently sees its global role as that of handling international disequilibrium through deflation and competitive devaluation.

The second general point is that criticism of the role of the IMF might appear as criticism of it as an institution, or even of its officials. While there is no doubt that the specific contents of an IMF package are likely to be influenced by the views of the officials involved in its formulation, it is also clear that they are constrained by the views of the most powerful members of the Fund, the larger industrial nations, who are ultimately responsible for the policies adopted by the Fund.

127

Brian Van Arkadie

It is the practice of the Fund to conduct its business in a highly confidential manner, rendering analysis of the role of the Fund by outside commentators quite difficult. Much of the comment in this paper relates to specific proposals of the Fund in September 1981, which are a matter of public record following disclosure in the Tanzanian National Assembly. All the indications are that those proposals represent the Fund's thinking in relation to Tanzania. The issues at stake are important enough to justify discussion of the proposals, even in the absence of a fuller analysis from the Fund motivating its position. An effort is made to explore the reasoning that is believed to lie behind that position; it is hoped that the description is not a parody of IMF thinking.

THE ORIGINS AND NATURE OF THE TANZANIAN CRISIS

The African continent is now facing an extended economic crisis. This has been fully recognised at the international level by, for example, the IBRD Report [*1981*] (the so-called Berg report) and by the DAC report [*OECD, 1980*), which concentrated on the special problems of sub-Saharan Africa.

Moreover in the last two years, as the international economic crisis has worsened, the African countries have proved to be especially vulnerable. A crucial manifestation of the crisis is formed by the balance of payments difficulties, which for most countries are the worst they ever have faced, and which have placed their economies in a vice imposed on the one side by continuing dependence on imports and on the other by the extreme shortage of foreign exchange.

Tanzania, in its current predicament, shares many of its problems with the rest of Africa. There are significant factors, however, which make it different. Thus, its vulnerability results from the same factors of dependence on primary commodity markets, climatic uncertainties and mediocre agricultural performance. Its particular character results from its special institutional structure and its rather good performance in provision of many basic social services, as demonstrated in the recent JASPA/ILO Report *Basic Needs in Danger.*[1]

To provide the setting to the discussion, I will sketch with a

128

broad brush the origins and nature of the current Tanzanian crisis. Tanzania had gone through a period of severe difficulty in the mid-1970s when the combined effects of the first oil price rise and a period of harvest failure had undermined economic performance and thrown the balance of payments into disarray. By 1978, as a result of a successful drive to expand food production, a boom in coffee and tea prices, and significant foreign assistance, Tanzania had weathered the crisis and seemed set to enter a new period of economic expansion.[2]

In the three following years, however, the economy went through a further battering, creating a far worse economic situation than that of the mid-1970s – partly because coming so soon after the earlier difficulties some of the reserves of self-confidence and resilience had already been eroded.

Briefly, during the period since 1978 the economy has been hit by the following events:

(i)   the war with Uganda, beginning at the end of 1978;

(ii)   adverse external economic conditions, starting with the end of the coffee and tea boom, followed in 1979-80 with the second oil price hike, and, in common with most of the rest of Africa, a further deterioration in the terms of trade in 1981-82 as recession in the OECD economies softened primary commodity markets;

(iii)   the break-up of the East African Community imposed significant economic burdens, particularly the cost of building-up transport services previously administered on an East African-wide basis;

(iv)   finally, and hopefully temporarily, the country was again hit by a spell of inadequate rain, resulting in two poor harvests (1980 and 1981).

The size of these short-term shocks and their coincidence meant that in almost any conceivable circumstances Tanzania would now be passing through a period of great economic difficulty. Looking back over the past decade, however, it is fair to say that vulnerability has been increased by certain underlying long-term weaknesses (and, in turn of course, the short-term difficulties have undermined the longer-term performance).

The three critical longer-term weaknesses in Tanzanian economic performance are:

129

(i)   poor agricultural performance, particularly in relation to export agriculture. The fact that 50 to 60 per cent of export earnings must now be allocated to petroleum imports as compared to 10 to 15 per cent a decade ago (for roughly the same quantity of petrol) is partly the result of price changes but also reflects a severe decline in the physical quantum of exports. The causes of this decline are discussed below;

(ii)   a high rate of industrial growth has failed to reduce import dependence (because of the high dependence on imported inputs) and has yet to make a significant impact on export performance;

(iii)   the parastatal (i.e. state) economic institutions which control key productive and marketing activities have a mixed record, indicating a major need to improve their performance.

The basic dilemma that Tanzania now faces is that between 50 and 60 per cent of export earnings go to pay for oil imports, and that imports now run at twice the level of export earnings despite restrictions on import levels which are so severe that capacity utilisation is constrained in all sectors and severe scarcities bring one sector or another of the economy to a halt each month.

It is fair to say that even in the absence of adverse external economic influences Tanzania would have major economic problems requiring solution – indeed, that will always be the case in a poor developing country. At the moment, however, the severity of the immediate economic crisis makes it difficult to tackle the fundamental tasks of improving agricultural performance, modifying industrial structure and improving parastatal efficiency.

The reason why it is difficult to tackle the longer-term structural problems is that the immediate impact of the crisis is to create a number of macro-imbalances which make it impossible for any particular part of the economy to work properly. The most important imbalance has already been mentioned – the imbalance on the external account. This is important in itself and it also feeds other crucial imbalances.

For example, since 1978 the fiscal and monetary situation has been in some disarray. Until 1978 Tanzania had a good record of maintaining a balanced recurrent budget and restrained monetary expansion. Indeed, until the explosion in world prices during the 1970s Tanzania had also maintained a remarkably stable price level. Since 1978, initially as a result of the war, the picture has changed, with the appearance of substantial deficits in the recurrent budget, acceleration in the growth of money supply and a substantially higher rate of inflation in Tanzania than could be explained by the behaviour of international prices.

The difficulty of recovering from this position is that the constraints on real output resulting from the exchange crisis (with much of industry working at 30 per cent capacity) has a depressing effect on the budget because of the impact on sales tax receipts and on parastatal profits (and losses).

The impact of the foreign exchange crisis can also be seen in the imbalance which has emerged between directly productive and service activities – as directly productive activity has declined, the balance in the economy has shifted sharply in favour of the service sectors.

Interrelated with these problems is a further imbalance between official and illicit economic activity. The economic system which has been fashioned in Tanzania could roughly be described as a managed market economy, with financial institutions and large-scale marketing (including export marketing) under public ownership, with an extensive public role in the industrial sector, but with continuing private involvement in construction, road transport, industry and local distribution. Moreover, the core of the economy continues to be smallholder farming. To manage this system the government has attempted to regulate wages and prices. Prices for the most important annual crops are set, for example, ahead of the planting period for the coming season. A wide range of prices are in principle controlled in the domestic market based on the assessment of a reasonable supply price under normal operating conditions. While no doubt this system is always likely to be less than perfect, under 'normal' conditions it would provide the basis for a roughly effective decentralised economic management system. Even under crisis conditions, the system has continued to do some tasks well – such as ensuring that scarce goods do get to the regions.

However, the system has come under two sorts of stress. While any system of price regulation is likely to result in some

131

unintended imbalances, under recent conditions of goods famine a fairly general gap emerges between the 'normal' supply price and a market clearing price, as consumers chase fewer and fewer goods. Parallel markets emerge, generating a circuit of income which falls outside the tax system. Moreover, inflation undermines the intended incentive effects of prices set ahead of time (notably agricultural prices).

Interrelated with the imbalances already mentioned, is that which has emerged between the level of new capital formation and the capacity to utilise and maintain the existing capital stock. New capital formation has been at higher levels than might be expected given the levels of idle capacity in the economy. This is, of course, not necessarily a bad thing. New investment which breaks existing bottlenecks may raise the utilisation of existing capital stock, and some longer-term investments will be justified in order to avoid the emergence of new capacity constraints in the future. Nevertheless, it is the case that capital formation has been maintained at too high a level given the severity of the short-term crisis. This is for two reasons. On the one hand, over the years government has tended to identify the development effort with capital formation, and is therefore not keen to reduce development spending. On the other hand, much of the development budget has been aid financed. While some donors – notably the Dutch and the Scandinavians – have shown commendable realism and flexibility in shifting aid to import support and recurrent needs, this flexibility has its limits – so that reductions in development spending only to a limited degree release resources for recurrent purposes.

THE IMF PROPOSALS

This brings the discussion to the IMF. For poor countries which have little possibility to place their public debt in private capital markets, the main possible source of balance of payments support, untied to capital projects, is the IMF. This dependency is reinforced because World Bank willingness to undertake structural adjustment programme support is likely to be positively influenced by agreement between the country in question and the Fund, necessarily so as the Bank cannot be seen to be offering itself as an alternative to the Fund.

Moreover, not only does the IMF have money available in the form and amounts required but, having described Tanzania's immediate problems of short-term macroeconomic management, it should properly be the IMF which should be the repository of expert technical advice in these matters.

Before going on to discuss the IMF prescription in the Tanzanian circumstance, it may be worthwhile making some general points about the issue of conditionality. The case of conditionality for higher tranche drawing on IMF facilities is unchallengeable on grounds of general principle, unless one were to suppose that the IMF were to play the role of international Santa Claus. Moreover, given the problems the IMF is expected to respond to, it is surely only reasonable that conditionality should apply to macro-policy instruments and broad measures of macro-performance, particularly those directly related to the balance of payments, along with other fiscal and monetary variables which can plausibly be argued to have a strong bearing on balance of payments performance.

A slightly cynical view might even suppose that the apparent loss of sovereignty might be of some unadmitted advantage to local political leaders in some circumstances, providing a scapegoat for necessary but unpopular measures. A recent study of IMF lending has identified a couple of cases where this was apparently the main motivation for IMF borrowing.

While the inevitability of conditionality can be agreed, there can be no simple conclusion regarding the appropriate conditions in particular instances. One fundamental problem may be posed as follows. This book demonstrates that among a selection of economists, more or less of goodwill and more or less professionally competent, there is no basic agreement about the appropriate policies to be pursued in face of macroeconomic difficulties – and this is even so amongst that range of opinion which could broadly be described as mainstream establishment within the OECD countries. Faced with this situation, governments can choose the advice they take – but they cannot choose the IMF they go to. The IMF, although no doubt an exponent of competition in all its forms, wields a virtual monopoly in the role it plays with respect to the poorer countries who have no significant access to private international capital markets. For the industrialised countries, with a few notable exceptions, the IMF role in recent years has been at most marginal to their domestic policy concerns, and even from the point of view of informed opinion, the details of IMF policy and *modus operandi* can easily remain an essentially esoteric matter.

Not so for the poor countries. They find that in the current moment the IMF becomes quite central to their policy concerns. It therefore becomes crucial which particular views from the wide range of Western establishment views are incorporated into IMF conditions.

Broadly, the position which has been identified as the 'IMF' position in relation to management of balance of payments difficulties could be described as:

(i)   being based on the monetary explanation of the balance of payments. That is, the key link between the balance of payments performance and domestic policy is through the money supply and that balance of payments disequilibrium should be adjusted through monetary restraint (based on the so-called 'Polak model');[3]

(ii)   the IMF has also been associated with the active use of exchange rate adjustment (i.e. devaluation) as an adjustment tool;

(iii)   the IMF approach is essentially a short-term approach with performance being judged, both for reasons of practice and principle, by the behaviour of relatively few aggregate indicators, money supply and credit ceilings often featuring as the most important.

There is now a large (and fast growing) literature on IMF conditionality discussing the relevance of the IMF approach. I do not intend to review or add to that literature, except to note three points:

(i)   when the sources of imbalance are essentially external, an adjustment process which emphasises restraint on demand may well adjust the balance of payments but at heavy deflationary cost;

(ii)   when the requirement for structural adjustment over the longer term involves significant shifts between sectors and

134

institutional changes, it is to be doubted that a limited number of macro-tools can do the trick;

(iii) the time horizon for structural adjustment of the kind now required in the current African crisis is likely to be considerably longer than that needed to restore a balance of payments disequilibrium resulting primarily from failures in domestic demand management. To a degree the IMF has attempted to accommodate to the need for longer period programmes by undertaking three-year arrangements, but in the past year has moved back to the use of a one-year arrangement as the norm.

In examining the specifics of a practical case as we now are, however, there are only limited returns to be gained from discussion of the 'IMF' model of exchange rate adjustment or IMF practice in general. A recent study of the IMF [*Killick, 1981*] indicates a range of practice, within certain basic limits, in relation to the preconditions and performance criteria attached to upper-tranche stand-by arrangements and access to extended fund facilities. Devaluation appears much less often than might be expected – in only a quarter of cases in the period 1973-78 were such arrangements associated with devaluation, for example – and credit ceilings were a more general condition. The variation in conditions reflects not only the variations in the nature of the economic situation of the country in question, but also the views of the particular IMF mission and the influence of powerful members of the Executive Board.

Turning now to the IMF and the current Tanzanian situation, we find a somewhat tortuous story which is difficult to summarise with fairness to all parties, particularly because of the difficulties inherent in analysing international negotiations – participants will not be without bias while outsiders will find it difficult to obtain information about, and to interpret the nuances of, complex discussions. To summarise main events briefly: in 1979 an attempt to negotiate a major programme led to an acrimonious breakdown following the presentation of an IMF package involving substantial devaluation, a wage freeze, abolition of price control, higher interest rates, relaxation of import controls and reduction in real government expenditure. In 1980 a new IMF team negotiated a three-year stand-by of

SDR 195 million, its main features involving the postponement of decisions on the exchange rate question until 1981 (following a Bank of Tanzania/IMF study), the imposition of credit ceilings for government borrowing and total credit formation, and a reduction in external commercial arrears. Before the year was out the programme fell apart because of a lack of realism regarding the lags between financing and output (and therefore tax) response, an underestimation of accumulated arrears, and a failure of World Bank structural adjustment lending to materialise of the size and speed envisaged.

This brings us to 1981. Negotiations took place with an IMF mission under new leadership. Discussions in March and July failed to reach agreement. Then, in September, the IMF submitted a confidential memorandum outlining a possible financial programme. The most controversial elements of the IMF proposals were made public by the Minister of Planning in answering a question in the Bunge (Parliament) on 20 October 1981. To summarise the Minister's statement, the proposals included:

(i)   *Devaluation* moving from Sh. 8.30 to the dollar to the range Sh. 16-20, to be followed by monthly adjustments reflecting Tanzanian inflation (or by a floating system) with maintenance of a unitary exchange rate;

(ii)   *Overall deficit* to be reduced to Sh. 4.5-5 billion (about 15 per cent of GDP), bank financing to Sh. 2-2.5 billion (14 per cent of initial money stock);

(iii)   There were to be *no wage increases* in the first year of the programme;

(iv)   *Parastatals* were to operate 'commercially sound' policies, eliminating the need for budget support; in particular the retail official price of sembe (maize meal – the preferred staple food) was to increase more than threefold to Sh. 8 per kilo, and the prices of gasoline and oil were to be raised to avoid subsidies on petroleum products;

(v)   *Interest rates* were to be raised to levels at which deposit rates would be positive in real terms and lending rates would avoid the need of subsidies;

(vi)   *Farm incentives* were to be improved – producer prices were to be raised 75 to 80 per cent and to be adjusted in future to cost of living changes; at the same time, import controls on essential inputs were to be removed – by liberalising price control and adopting a single licensing system.

How far this proposal represented an IMF view of a desirable final package, or was rather a negotiating position from which the IMF would have been willing to move to find middle ground cannot be said, for that was for the moment the end of negotiations – there was no formal break but for the subsequent seven months they were not resumed. One hopes, in fact, that the IMF would be willing to shift to new ground in subsequent discussions; any commont on *the* IMF position in relation to the current Tanzanian crisis may not reflect what might emerge in subsequent discussions.

Any realistic evaluation of policy must be compared with some realistic alternative; in the following discussion the IMF approach is contrasted at a number of points with an alternative approach to structural adjustment; an approach which, it is believed, is preferable in that it is more gradual and therefore more realistic, more comprehensive and more sensitive to distributional goals. As such, it is close to the position actually adopted by the Tanzanian Government in its own programme.[4]

In the IMF stance towards Tanzania in this period one can observe three general characteristics which define and limit the nature of the solution they offer:
(i) the predilection for a few powerful measures (which places great weight – probably too much – on a few policy instruments);
(ii) an exclusive emphasis on market policy instruments;
(iii) an emphasis on sharp shocks expected to have substantial results in the short period.

One implication of the IMF position seems to be that the managed mixed economy is inherently less satisfactory than a more private and laissez-faire regime, and that movements towards the latter should be an important element in any programme.

This has three negative results:
(i) advice is given which may be largely irrelevant in the institutional setting as it is;
(ii) a number of non-market policy measures appropriate to the particular institutional setting are neglected;
(iii) by locating sensible enough advice about the use of

particular policy instruments in such unsatisfactory packages, even that advice may be rendered suspect.

In essence, the spirit behind the IMF position seems to be not so much how to make the Tanzanian system work, but rather how to move towards its replacement by a quite different model.

A CRITICAL REVIEW OF THE IMF PROPOSALS

The nature of the differences in approach between the IMF and a more flexible and comprehensive structural adjustment strategy can be summarised briefly under four heads: the scope of policy measures; magnitudes of movements in key variables; timing; implied economic strategy.

Scope

The IMF concentration on relatively few policy instruments (in this case the exchange rate, farm prices, food prices and interest rates in particular) may be seen to flow from two considerations:

(i)   the practical need to define certain clear and measurable conditions as a part of any package;

(ii)   a belief that the government should essentially concern itself with macroeconomic equilibrium, leaving market forces to determine microeconomic allocation decisions.

This approach can be argued to have three weaknesses from the Tanzanian point of view:

(i)   in order to make a plausible case that the desired result will be achieved through the use of a very limited set of tools, very large movements in the chosen variables are advocated; the use of a wider mixture of policy instruments does not place so much weight on the chosen IMF instruments; the adoption of a more comprehensive approach allows for a more modest adjustment in the 'IMF' instruments;

(ii)   by concentrating on the presumed effects of these instruments there is a danger of over-simplification of problems (e.g. of the agricultural sector); an alternative approach should place proper weight on institutional factors;

(iii)   a doctrinal over-emphasis on the market and against subsidies limits the capacity of the government to achieve

138

desired distributional objectives; an alternative approach would defend stated Tanzanian goals but in a pragmatic fashion.

Magnitudes in the Movement of Key Variables

The IMF seeks very large movements in such variables as the exchange rate and farm prices. No doubt in justification it would be argued that the magnitude of the movement sought merely reflects the degree to which the system is in disequilibrium. As was noted above, however, large movements also may result from the limited range of instruments chosen and from the speed of adjustment sought.

The difficulty with the pursuit of such large changes goes to the root of problems of macroeconomic management. The case for exchange rate adjustment rests on the need to adjust the real exchange rate for the unintended effects of inflation in recent years. However, inflation itself results from the failure of policy to achieve given real targets by pursuing given monetary goals. The achievement of a desired change in the real exchange rate is not necessarily achieved by an immediate move in the money exchange rate by the desired amount.

The reason for this is as follows. The function of a change in the exchange rate in the Tanzanian case is to facilitate an increase in real resources allocated to the export sector (international terms of trade broadly being determined externally). In the absence of an injection of resources, that real transfer can only occur if the real resources available to other sectors are reduced. (This is not dissimilar to the situation in industrial economies in which devaluation is fundamentally a mechanism for reducing real wage rates, and only works insofar as that reduction is accepted.)

If the non-export sectors cannot, or will not, release real resources to the export sector, the effect of the devaluation will be wiped out by a round of inflationary price, wage and budgetary increases in other sectors. It may well be possible to assimilate modest shifts without provoking resistance, where very large shifts are likely to be followed by pressures leading to across-the-board compensatory wage and price adjustments, whatever the initial policy intention. Because of this, a more

139

gradual alternative might be a surer way of eventually achieving a desired adjustment in the real exchange rate, and would almost certainly be less likely to lead to the unleashing of additional inflationary forces of the kind which have become endemic in the Latin American economies. (In this regard, when the large exchange rate adjustment is added to proposals to index key prices and introduce positive real interest, the intent seems to be to institutionalise inflation rather than to correct it.)

After all, if the economy were able to sustain large resource transfers it would also be possible to subsidise agricultural exports through non-inflationary budgetary means; the difficulty in so doing, which arises because of the difficulties of squeezing revenues from other sectors, provides one of the most powerful arguments for the more indirect approach through devaluation – but also indicates the limits of such a policy. The underlying constraint is a real one both in an economic and a political sense.

In relation to the magnitude of the exchange rate adjustment favoured by the IMF there is also another problem. The desired adjustment implied by their targets apparently aims to accommodate the restoration of the real value of export producer prices to earlier levels, compensating both for the effects of relative inflation rates (a reasonable enough objective) and for negative shifts in the international terms of trade. The justification for the latter element in the adjustment is unclear. If the export price decline is permanent, then good neo-classical reasoning suggests that producer prices should reflect the shift; if cyclical, then the exchange rate is surely not the appropriate tool for price stabilisation.

Timing

The IMF seeks major exchange rate and price moves before the injection of resource transfers and the resulting output expansion, the argument being that only then will resource inflows be utilised at 'realistic' prices. The more gradual approach argues that sharp price changes prior to the release of additional resources are likely to be self-defeating, engendering further windfall gains and inflationary pressures leaving the expected allocation efficiency benefits uncertain. The counter-argument by the IMF that actual prices paid by the end user already reflect real scarcities (i.e. parallel market prices are much higher than official prices) in fact blunts its own argument for the allocative efficiency of official price adjustments, but also underestimates the degree to which official price controls do work and provide a check on the inflationary process.

The argument for a sequence in which the foreign exchange constraint is eased and output is increased *pari passu* with exchange rate and price adjustment follows on from the previous analysis, suggesting that for the real price change to stick, resource transfers must be accepted by the system; transfers are obviously easier when resources are expanding.

Another aspect of timing is the length of the expected adjustment process. The IMF approach involves an initial shock treatment in response to which swift improvement in performance, even within the year, is hoped for. This approach may be realistic, even if not optimal, in situations in which external disequilibrium results from excessive levels of domestic aggregate demand, in which case sharp deflationary measures might be swiftly translated into improvements in the external trade account. No one claims that this is the case in Tanzania, where the problem is not one of demand management so much as that of generating the funds to sustain desirable import levels. Given the degree to which imports have already been squeezed, further reductions would be likely to result in declines in exports, whatever the domestic policy mix.

Movement towards something like a satisfactory balance of payments situation requires:
(i)   a restoration in the output of exported commodities – the conditions necessary for that to be achieved are discussed below, but realistically there is no reason to suppose that this corner can be turned in one or even two years;
(ii)   recovery in export prices; the floor in the downward movement in world commodities apparently has not yet been reached. This is a matter over which Tanzania has no control. In the absence of improvements in the external economic environment there is a limit to which Tanzania and other African countries can recover.

This implies that substantial balance of payments support

should be envisaged for at least three years and, if the world crisis continues, maybe longer.

If such finance is not available then it is unlikely that either an IMF-type programme or a more gradual adjustment approach would work. In that circumstance it may be necessary to pursue more drastic measures to live with an extreme foreign exchange constraint for some years.

Strategy

The broad commitment to the primacy of market forces which seems to motivate IMF thinking to a large degree obviates the need for any more specific views regarding economic strategy. In the case of its prescription for Tanzania, however, the Fund does go one major step further, in concentrating on large increases in producer prices for agricultural exports.

The internal coherence of the proposed IMF package rests on three logical steps:
(i)   that economic decisions are best dictated by market forces;
(ii)   that free play of market forces would demonstrate the comparative advantage of specialisation in export agriculture; and
(iii)   that the supply response of export agriculture to price incentives can be expected to be highly elastic.

This view is also influential within the World Bank – and is applied on an African-wide basis in the Berg Report.

Before raising some questions regarding this line of argument, it is important to accept a partial truth in each step in the argument.

The necessity of placing increased emphasis on market instruments to achieve policy instruments has been emphasised in the Tanzanian Structural Adjustment Programme. For the policy maker, however, the market is a useful servant but a poor master. The current crisis has demonstrated the need for significant policy reform but this is far from suggesting that there is any virtue in the abandonment of efforts to change the structure of the economy and influence the distribution of income, consumption and wealth.

The emphasis on agricultural exports raises issues going beyond the scope of a discussion of short-term macroeconomic

142

management. There can be no question that the most damaging failure in economic performance in the 1970s has been in relation to agriculture and that a prime task of any policy package needs to be the reversal of recent declines in export performance. It can also be agreed that improved incentives are necessary. However, this leaves a number of key questions unanswered (and, indeed, unasked).

First, of course, the current behaviour of world markets by no means lends unequivocal support for the concentration of efforts on traditional agricultural exports, particularly as a collective strategy for the traditional exporters (a legitimate point, as the multilaterals tend to hawk the same advice throughout the Third World).

Second, certain aspects of the crisis of the 1970s raise more fundamental doubts about the wisdom of dependence on agricultural exports. From the data now available it is evident that the downturn in agricultural export performance came in the early 1970s. Many factors coincided in that period which could have contributed to the decline, but certainly one factor was the emergence of considerable difficulties in meeting Tanzania's food requirements. Initially this was associated with two years of bad weather resulting in poor harvests, but subsequently (despite two good years in which virtual self-sufficiency was restored) an endemic problem has emerged not only of supplying food to fast growing urban areas, but also of providing food in certain cash crop zones, such as the cotton zone of Mwanza and Shinyanga. The underlying problem is that high population growth has not been matched by an increase in productivity in food crop production. Moreover, the clearest evidence of strong price responsiveness on the part of farmers is in relation to cross-elasticity of supply between food crops and export crops.

Much of the growth in agricultural exports in the 1960s was at the extensive margin. Whether such growth can be reproduced in the 1980s as a response to price incentives in the face of food supply difficulties without significant breakthroughs in agricultural productivity is one question to be addressed; more alarmingly, what would be the consequences of accelerated export growth achieved at the expense of food production? Put baldly, with its high population growth rate and often fragile

143

rural environment, is Africa's future comparative advantage in agricultural exports self-evident?

In immediate practical terms, the Tanzanian situation varies from region to region and crop to crop; probably for some regions and export crops improvement could be achieved without losses in food output.

If such growth is feasible within the available technologies, how far can it be achieved through the price incentive instrument? The limits on the possible range in which incentives can be moved have already been mentioned – ultimately real goods have to come from somewhere.

Moreover, even if improved incentives are a necessary condition for improved performance, in most cases they are unlikely to be sufficient,[5] just as the origins of the decline were not merely a matter of declining incentives (indeed it could be argued that the particularly severe declines in incentives resulted from a deterioration in export performance rather than vice versa). Other factors, such as institutional weaknesses in marketing (including the abolition of the cooperatives and inadequacies of the parastatal marketing authorities) resulting in failures to purchase the crop, to supply inputs and to pay promptly, inadequacies in research and extension, villagisation (particularly in the case of cashews), public takeover of large-scale farms (particularly sisal), disease and soil fertility problems, all took their toll. Issues related to institutional change in marketing and extension services and to the allocation of resources as between price increases, investment in infrastructure (e.g. roads), investment in agriculture itself or in research, and the provision of incentive goods are complicated, and perhaps have been resolved badly enough in the past to lend some appeal to the simple cry for a massive increase in incentives. Unfortunately, however, incentives are only likely to be sufficiently effective as an element in a more complex package.

Perhaps an hypothesis which deserves exploration in the light of the difficult problems facing agriculture, and alongside the fact that the countries which have done relatively better over the past two decades are those which have diversified their export base, is that very high priority should be given to the generation of industrial exports.

It is doubtful whether the Tanzanian Structural Adjustment

Programme has itself yet come to terms with the institutional improvements required for accelerated agricultural growth or the necessary measures for export diversification, but ultimately, successful adjustment will require that those problems be tackled.

The importance the IMF has given to the interest rate issue is another indication of the gap between IMF strategy and Tanzanian reality, where the proposed policy emphasis cannot but seem more a matter of doctrine than of pragmatic judgement.

On the proposal to institute positive real interest rates (implying interest rates around 30 per cent as compared with around 10 per cent at present) there are two objections. In an economy where most lending, and also a good deal of borrowing, is by public institutions, the interest rate has a limited function as an allocation device; the immediate effect would be to create further disarray in the finance of crop authorities and meaningless surpluses in the financial parastatals. Even if a case could be made for shifting to the use of the interest rate as an active allocation device among public institutions, there is no evidence that this would have an impact on short-term adjustment, justifying its inclusion in an IMF package. Moreover, a move to a regime of high nominal interest rates combined with floating or crawling exchange rates would imply an acceptance of inflation as an endemic characteristic of the Tanzanian economy, which one must learn to live with, rather than a temporary phenomenon which can be eliminated.

Despite all these points, it can be argued that one element of monetarist orthodoxy is extremely pertinent to Tanzanian circumstances. An important element of the deterioration in the Tanzanian situation is the deterioration in the budgetary situation. It is difficult to restore the balance in the recurrent budget and to check the growth in money supply, partly because of the fiscal effects of the foreign exchange crisis, but the negative effects of the lack of fiscal and monetary control must be recognised.

A quasi-planned managed market economy is less able to operate under conditions of endemic and serious inflation than a less controlled economy. If anything, the more planned the economy the greater the need for a certain fiscal orthodoxy. Government-induced inflation with all its unpredictable and uncontrolled effects demoralises efforts to plan and direct the economy.

Likewise, the need to improve parastatal performance is well taken but it is not evident (as seems implicit in the IMF position) that pricing policy lies at the root of the parastatal problem.

Finally, we may note the distributional aspects of the package. The freeze of nominal wages and the quite specific demand for an increase in food prices would place a more than proportionate part of the burden of adjustment on the shoulders of urban wage earners in a situation in which there is no evidence that they have done comparatively better than other groups (for example, farmers) during the crisis, or that these measures will have specific effects on the balance of payments (they might have effects on the budget but as any package would probably include overall budget ceilings these specific proposals would largely affect distribution within the budget).

SOME CONCLUSIONS

It is not surprising that the IMF takes no account of distributional factors or that its proposals are far from neutral in their effect. However, this does pose questions for bilateral aid donors, from whom the call has come for basic needs policies over the past decade and who have favoured Tanzania precisely because of its concern about the distributional aspects of development.

With the world in crisis, is distribution now to be ignored? Have the donor countries achieved a coherence between the views of development agencies which influence their aid programmes, and views on appropriate financial policies communicated to the IMF through the same governments' finance ministries and central banks?

Some of the issues discussed here will strike a resonant note to those familiar with the structuralist versus monetarist controversies in Latin America of twenty years ago; this may be not so much because of similarity between African conditions now and Latin American conditions then as because of the continuity in the IMF stance.

Apart from the specific position of the IMF in the spectrum

of professional economic views, IMF packages are characteristic of much purely economic analysis in believing in the efficacy of a few purely economic instruments if properly utilised. However, the nature and seriousness of the condition may be such that no cure will work which is based purely on the interpretation and manipulation of a few economic variables.

This does not mean that the IMF should extend its areas of conditionality and begin to involve itself in areas which it has always seen as outside its purview. The consequences of such a move would not necessarily be happy. It does mean, however, that in relation to its chosen areas of conditionality the IMF should have a great deal more humility in its advocacy of its preferred packages and a great deal more flexibility in considering a range of options.

The net result of the IMF-Tanzanian relationship over 1981-82 is that no viable agreement has been made so far and that, in relation to crucial issues such as the exchange rate, the IMF intervention can arguably be claimed to have postponed a moderate, sensible adjustment by demanding a change large enough to be uncertain in its consequences and, anyway, unacceptable in practice.

If we see the problem of policy improvement as one of improving the system and rationality of economic decision making, then a process of forcing a government to take its medicine, however nasty, has little virtue – policy changes thus made will not be incorporated in a fundamental sense but will just be seen as a necessary if temporary burden to be shouldered in return for the needed cash. Moreover, packages which increase political instability and throw doubts on the sovereignty of the recipient government are not ultimately conducive to the development of an effective and orderly economic policy system.

But perhaps most importantly, we must recognise that there are many alternative strategies of equal plausibility from an economic point of view but of varying appropriateness from an institutional or political point of view.

In these terms there are two alternative questions that can be asked when faced with the crisis condition of Tanzania. One is how can the occasion be used to shift the basic direction of Tanzanian development to a more open, private and uncontrol-

Brian Van Arkadie

led system. The other is how to improve Tanzanian performance while defending Tanzanian gains in terms of provision of basic needs and furthering stated Tanzanian goals of egalitarian development. The current economic crisis should not be the excuse for jettisoning concern for the fundamental purposes of economic development, at home or abroad, and particularly not in favour of policies which are of dubious effectiveness even in their own terms.

NOTES

1. Completed 1981. Publication forthcoming.
2. See Green, Rwegasira & Van Arkadie [*1981*]. In retrospect, that study ended on an over-optimistic note and under-estimated the degree to which poor economic performance had become endemic.
3. The original presentation of this model as well as some later developments of it are bundled in IMF [*1977*].
4. Structural Adjustment Programme for Tanzania, June 1982.
5. In fact there is no secure evidence on the magnitude of an overall supply response in agriculture to an increase in the general level of prices. Performance in relation to cashew nuts is at least equivocal. An increase in price of 175 per cent over the period 1979/80 to 1981/82 led to a positive response initially, but has been followed by a sharp falling-off in 1981/82, at best suggesting that there may be a considerable time lag before a sustained response can be expected, and probably indicating the need for a package of additional measures to improve the supply situation before a satisfactory supply response can be expected.

REFERENCES

Green, R. H., D. G. Rwegasira & B. Van Arkadie, 1980, *Economic Shocks and National Policy Making*, The Hague, Institute of Social Studies, Research Report No. 8.
IBRD, 1981, *Accelerated Development in Sub-Saharan Africa*, Washington.
IMF, 1977, *The Monetary Approach to the Balance of Payments*, Washington.
Killick, T., 1981, 'IMF Stabilisation Programmes in the Third World', *ODI Working Paper, No. 6.*
OECD, 1980, *Development Cooperation, Efforts and Policies of the Members of the Development Assistance Committee*, Report by J.R. Lewis, Paris, November.

IX
International Keynesianism –
A Solution to the World Crisis?
by *LAL JAYAWARDENA*

THE CONCEPT OF INTERNATIONAL KEYNESIANISM

It must be said at the outset that international Keynesianism is not a solution to the world crisis any more than monetarism provides a solution. Keynesianism can at best provide a partial solution in the restrictive context of established economic relationships between the Third World and the developed world as given by the prevailing linkages in respect of trade and financial flows. A solution to the world crisis, seen from a Third World standpoint, requires fundamental changes in these inter-relationships in order to reduce the impact on the Third World of policies that are essentially determined elsewhere and over which the Third World has little immediate control. It also implies far-reaching national social changes, without· which international action may be self-defeating. These changes are encapsulated in the call for structural change contained in the New International Economic Order Resolutions of the United Nations. An essential goal of these changes is to establish within the Third World a process of self-reliant development which will render it less vulnerable to the impact of decisions that are outside its control.

The recent UNCTAD Trade and Development Report [*1981*] represents an attempt to indicate the scale of self-reliant effort needed in the Third World if it is to go beyond the confines set for it by prevailing linkages between GDP growth in the two

149

worlds. The starting point for UNCTAD's analysis is the World Bank's low projection for the period 1980-90 of a 2.8 per cent annual GDP growth rate for the developed market economies, associated with an average GDP growth for the developing countries of 4.6 per cent. UNCTAD, being rightly more pessimistic, scales down these projections to an average of 2.4 per cent and 4.2 per cent respectively. As long as international steps are not taken to break this dependence, there is little prospect of Third World countries growing at the minimum 'socially necessary' rate required to prevent further increases in their already high unemployment rates. In UNCTAD's view, the Third World needs to grow by at least 6.3 per cent per annum in the 1980s, rising to nearly seven per cent per annum by the 1990s. This therefore requires an appropriate loosening of the linkages between the developing and the developed world.

The set of arguments denoted by International Keynesianism is necessarily limited to the much less ambitious objective of accepting prevailing linkages between the two worlds. A key premise is that these linkages have been strengthened during the past 20 years to the point where a demand stimulus emanating from the Third World can also serve as an engine of growth for the developed market economies, with mutually reinforcing feedback effects for the world economy as a whole. Depending on the sectoral direction of resource transfers needed for the stimulus, these linkages can be strengthened or loosened.

Two supporting premises of this argument are the following. First, that any such demand stimulus operating in the context of the deflationary impact of OPEC oil price increases is necessarily non-inflationary. Second, that the alternative of a reflationary stimulus *confined directly* to the economies of the North and not fed back via the South, encounters structural mismatches between supply and demand which make it both ineffective and inflationary. The point is that the slack capacities requiring stimulus in the North are in key export sectors which are ideally equipped to supply the infrastructural needs of early accelerated growth in the South, for example, the engineering, transport and power development sectors; and that the pattern of incremental demand resulting from direct reflation within the North involves a greater inflationary risk because domestic expenditures may fall on the 'wrong' sectors. Further, the multiplier effects of a stimulus via the South are likely to be reinforced by superior accelerator effects in inducing invest-ment, as is explicitly envisaged in one of the massive transfer proposals considered below, namely that of Masaki Nakajima. Such accelerator effects are clearly stronger in the context of global expansion than of contradiction.[1]

To outline the argument, let me repeat the statement made by Roy Jenkins in his Jean Monnet lecture which revived public discussion of the European Monetary system:

> We also need to view the present economic recession in a longer-term perspective. The extent and persistence of unemployment can no longer be seen as an exceptionally low and long bottom to the business cycle. To restore full employment requires a new impulse on a historic scale. We require a new driving force comparable with the major re-juvenations of the past two hundred years; the industrial revolution itself, the onset of the railway age, the impact of Keynes, the need for post-war reconstruction, the spread of what were previously regarded as middle class standards to the mass of population in the industrial countries. I believe that the needs of the Third World have a major part to play here. Two sources of new growth have in the past sometimes come together, the one world-wide and the other regional [*Jenkins, 1977: 17*].

At their Arusha meeting in early 1979, the Group of 77 formulated their demands prior to commencement of UNCTAD V in Manila in broadly similar terms [*UNCTAD 1979: 50*]. The Arusha Programme for Collective Self-Reliance constituted a political landmark in the international discussion of what has since come to be known as 'Massive Resource Transfer'. First, the call for a 'massive transfer' to developing countries in the cause of promoting global economic recovery ceased to be the exclusive concern of a few isolated individuals or of countries, and became the political platform of the Group of 77. Second, broad orders of magnitude were specified for the transfer: 'an initial additional financial transfer in the range of $35 to 50 billion'. Third, the Arusha Declaration was significant in con-tending that the massive transfer mechanism 'should in no way prejudice the expansion of ODA to meet accepted international

151

targets'. The Group of 77 was in fact urging the exploration of more automatic resource transfer mechanisms than are envisaged today, anticipating the suggestions in the Brandt Commission Report for international taxation.

Finally, the Arusha meeting spelt out the mechanism by which to bring about such a massive transfer, and the broad purposes to which the amounts might be devoted: 'The mechanism would analytically imply the raising under the collective guarantee of the international community of monies in international capital markets and their disbursement to developing countries over a long term period with an interest subsidy element as appropriate in the form of both project and programme lending for structural change.' The developing countries argued that in this regard, 'special attention should be given to the needs of the least developed and the most seriously affected countries.' The revenues accruing from donor country budgets could serve to finance interest subsidy expenditures needed to enable monies to be lent at below market rates to the poorer developing countries.

The significance of specifying the detail and purpose of the mechanism was threefold. First, it sought to present the argument for 'massive transfers' in a manner that would not impose a burden on the fiscal budgets of developed donor countries, emphasising the tapping of liquidity available in the world's capital markets. Second, in linking the concept of 'massive transfers' with an interest subsidy element permitting lending to *all* developing countries, the Group of 77 in effect erased any nuance of conferring an exclusive benefit on middle income developing countries. Third, in emphasising programme lending and tapping international capital markets, the Group of 77's formulation became the precursor of the Brandt Commission's subsequent argument in favour of a World Development Fund.

In key respects, the Brandt Commission's approach completed the edifice envisaged at Arusha. Its institutional device, the World Development Fund, proved to be nothing more than a specific application of the Arusha principle of tapping international capital markets. The detailed financial structure elaborated in the Brandt Commission papers [*IBIDI, 1981: 649-51*] was conceived on a scale of 120 billion in current dollars, of which six billion dollars would constitute paid-in capital with the balance being raised in international capital markets under the collective guarantee of the Fund's membership. This scale of funding was thought sufficient to ensure adequate programme lending and mineral and energy finance for the first seven years of operation of the World Development Fund, building up to an annual transfer of 20 billion dollars by the end of that period.

The analytical underpinnings to what is today a political argument for 'massive resource transfer' are derived primarily from the financial magnitudes needed to address the problems of structural change in developing countries, but are also rooted in the recessionary implications of the oil price increases of the last decade. It is in this latter context that the International Keynesian element in the argument has emerged. Perhaps the earliest analysis is that of Holsen and Waelbroeck [*1976: 175*], which explored the implications for developed country growth of the recycling of some 11 billion dollars-worth of OPEC surpluses to middle income developing countries, and argued that this had the effect of increasing aggregate demand in developed countries by six per cent and of enabling the borrowing countries to increase their GNP by seven per cent as against the zero growth that would have resulted in the absence of borrowings. The study argued that the financing of developing country deficits had sustained developed country demand to a degree equivalent to a 'vigorous German demand expansion'. The massive transfers that occurred merely offset the recessionary impact of a sharp rise in the price of oil, resulting in the immediate substantial increase in world savings.

The argument for massive transfer in the context of the second round of oil price increases is that, just as in the early 1970s when massive transfers through the private banking system had alleviated recession, an equivalent mechanism might now be needed to bring about the efficient recycling of financial surpluses. Any weakening in the capacity of private banks to play an effective recycling role must be offset by some form of official buttressing of the process if recessionary pressures are to be alleviated. In the context of an oil price increase, transfers are profoundly non-inflationary, and there

153

can be no question that better recycling will increase inflation. The argument is in no way invalidated in today's 'softer' oil price context because the emerging surplus countries, Japan and Germany, also have to look to a weakened banking system.

The point I have been making can be made more formally by drawing on the Report of a Commonwealth Group of Experts of which I was a member:

> It is a truism that the sum of the balance of payments surpluses and deficits on the current account of all countries must be zero. In other words, when there are current account surpluses (such as those run by OPEC today) [parenthetically, they used to be run not so long ago by the Federal Republic of Germany and Japan and the same reasoning applies – both then and when they re-emerge in the context of OPEC's current misfortunes] there are counterpart deficits that will have been financed and which exactly equal the surpluses. This equality obtains *ex-post* in any single year's accounting; in fact, it only indicates that the surpluses will have been lent or 'recycled' to finance the deficits that actually occur.
>
> These deficits will be diminished if the surplus countries can expand their imports either by boosting domestic activity or by allowing their rates of exchange to appreciate. But if there is no such relief to the strain on the financing mechanism, and if the mechanism is ineffective in permitting deficit countries to obtain finance from abroad, adjustment can take place only through a decline in economic activity, concentrated on the deficit countries but reacting throughout the system and bringing about an all-round curtailment of trade. The system will settle in balance at whatever level is required to balance the surpluses with the deficits that can be financed. In the 1970s, all these three processes, the lending of surpluses, the increase of imports into the surplus countries, and a reduction in the level of economic activity, were at work [*Arndt et al., 1980: 16*].

That Commonwealth Report dealt with each of these processes, but I wish to emphasise here that since the first two processes will be working less efficiently in the 1980s, the main adjustment will occur through a reduction in the level of global economic activity unless remedial action is taken. This is primarily because sluggish aid flows and the recycling difficulties encountered by private banks will limit the financing of balance of payments deficits, and because the absorptive capacity of many OPEC surplus countries for additional imports is expected to decline.

The anticipated diminution of the OPEC surplus and its substitution by, say, Japanese and German surpluses, is not likely to change the recessionary outlook immediately since these other surpluses will emerge only to the extent to which already weakened recycling processes will have financed the counterpart deficits. The point is that the potential is there for reduced Third World oil deficits to free import purchasing power, which will benefit developed country exports and could spark off a circle of recovery.

The principal transmission mechanism for recession or recovery is, of course, the potential of developing country import capacity, with its feedback effects on the exports of developed economies. The significance of Third World markets has been pointed out in a recent European Commission study.

In fact, the Third World is the Community's principal customer and in 1977 37.6 per cent of our exports went to the developing countries compared with 12.5 per cent to the United States and 9 per cent to the Eastern State trading countries. Only our exports to the North European countries reach comparable figures, accounting for 22 per cent of our total exports.

The most dynamic export markets within the developing countries are the OPEC countries. This is mainly due to the increase in oil prices and the enormous transfer of income ensuing therefrom. Since 1973, the share of exports to OPEC countries has more than doubled, from 8.2. per cent in 1973 to 18.1 per cent of total exports in 1977. Even the non-oil producing developing countries present more reliable and dynamic outlets than the industrialised countries. Had the developing countries followed the example of the industrialised countries after 1973, by cutting back both their growth and imports to adjust to the oil price increases, the recession in the industrialised countries would have been far more serious. The figures for 1975, when our economies reached their lowest point, are particularly striking. While Community exports to the United States fell by 17 per cent (in EUA terms) and those to the EFTA countries by 3.3. per cent, our exports to the developing countries increased by 25 per cent, those to the ACP countries alone by 33 per cent [*CEC, 1979: 53, 54*].

This point has recently been made more generally for the developing world as a whole:

Continued growth of developing countries is vital to the prosperity of developed countries. Last year exports to the non OPEC developing countries reached $180 billion, 34 per cent of all industrial exports (excluding the regional trade among West European countries and between the US and Canada). *The industrial countries should avoid an overly restrictive approach to developing country financing that would multiply recessionary forces affecting their own economies [Morgan Guaranty Trust, 1980: 2; emphasis added]*.

The source of this quotation is not the Brandt Commission, as many might suspect, but Wall Street. The point I have emphasised has a bearing on the precise mix of domestic policies which developed countries choose to adopt in controlling inflation, whether budget deficits are reduced through cutbacks in development assistance or not. Morgan Guaranty, on the other hand, make their point in the context of the recessionary implications of an expected slowing-down in private bank lending. They look primarily to the international financial institutions to take up this slack in demand, and argue for a restoration of the IMF's role in the financing of developing country deficits, including the lengthening of maturities so as to correspond to the structural nature of deficits requiring financing. Specifically, Morgan Guaranty suggest that the conditions which inhibit countries from approaching the IMF on time ought to be relaxed, one way being to increase the proportion of IMF resources available at reduced or minimal conditionality. Second, Morgan Guaranty argue the case for turning the existing compensatory financing facility of the IMF into 'a more broadly defined terms of trade financing facility'.

This, I need hardly stress, is sound G24 doctrine.[2] What is interesting is the extent to which the IMF has moved into the territory of financing developing country deficits through modifications in its lending policies in partial response to G24 criticisms. In effect, the IMF has substituted in some measure for the previous recycling role of private banks, having replenished its liquidity with its major Saudi borrowing. IMF lending commitments to developing countries have risen to SDR 17 billion in 1981 as compared with SDR nine billion in 1980 and SDR three billion in 1979 [*IMF, 1982*]; it can thus be claimed that the official buttress to a weakened private banking system is in part provided by expanded IMF activities. But with disbursements lagging behind commitments, IMF funds have financed well under 10 per cent of the non-oil developing country current account deficits. In addition, a number of IMF standby arrangements have lapsed in recent months, bringing into question the effectiveness of the Fund's recycling role and raising the issue of alternative approaches, perhaps outside the Fund.

NEW WAYS FOR THE 1980s

The present lacunae in international facilities reinforce the mounting evidence that additional props to private bank lending are needed. In 1981, for example, in its submission on North-South issues to the Maastricht Summit, the European Commission was concerned about the threat to Community exports of a failure of Third World purchasing power. In my view, a good deal of the positive European attitude towards launching the proposed global round of negotiations is ultimately traceable to such concern; in its Maastricht submission, there is for the first time the recognition by the Commission that, as contrasted with the period after the first oil crisis, 'the private banking sector is no longer enough' [*European Commission, 1981*].

It is worth dwelling briefly on the reasons for this. There is a concern that, with the total developing country debt rising to around $500 billion and with servicing costs averaging 20 per cent of their export earnings, their access to banking credit will be inhibited. Second, there is concern that country limits are being approached by the banking system for an increasing number of developing countries. Since a very large proportion of bank lending is concentrated in a few countries – some 12 in number – the deflationary implications are serious. Third, banks are becoming concerned about the adequacy of their capital in relation to the total size of their deposits – a point specifically made in the Commonwealth Report. Finally, there is the problem of how far the process of banks borrowing short and lending long can be sustained if the confidence of short-term depositors such as OPEC is eroded by even a single banking crisis.

The prospect that the surpluses now requiring recycling may not be those of OPEC in no way eases the problems confronting the private banking system, whose capacity to continue with the process of 'massive transfer' is impeded by the consequences of its previous success. The question now is whether surrogates to the private banks' recycling role are available.

Collective Self-Reliance

In the first place, there is the opportunity to bypass the intermediation of the conventional private banking system by building-up independent Third World institutions. This may be in the private sector, as exemplified by the recent development of Arab banking institutions such as the Arab Banking Corporation. Ideally, however, this would need to be complemented by efforts at official intermediation. A proposal has been tabled by Venezuela and Algeria that the OPEC Fund be transformed into a full-fledged development institution with a substantially enhanced capital. A complementary proposal has been articulated by Sri Lanka at the South-South meeting held recently in Delhi, where I was privileged to represent my country [*Jayawardena, 1982*]. The proposal was that, if Third World collective self-reliance is to be given any meaning, co-operation must extend not only to concessional aid as in the past, but to commercially viable development and investment projects of mutual interest to both surplus developing and deficit developing countries. The bulk of the cash surplus available for disposition by OPEC countries during the period 1974-81 is held, according to IMF data [*IMF, 1982: 165*] in industrial countries and in Eurocurrency markets – some $402 billion out of a total of $475 billion. Over time, these surpluses have eroded through inflation. Any mechanism which can diversify this portfolio by creating opportunities for equity investment in the Third World, will serve both as a hedge against inflation for surplus countries and as a source of financing desirable real capital formation in deficit countries. This will be needed if linkages within the Third World are to be strengthened and the dependence of Third World growth on that of the developed market economies is to be lessened.

Based upon this perception of mutual interest, the investment institutions of the major surplus countries in the Gulf are already active in the promoting of joint ventures in developing countries, and are in the process of creating a joint Gulf Investment Authority. In this context, there is scope for a multilateral investment institution, established within the Third World, to take its own initiatives in the process of project identification and development. The willingness of such an institution to take up a modest equity interest in any particular project would encourage the participation of other Gulf investment agencies, and facilitate portfolio diversification. Such a Southern investment institution can also combine facilities for providing export credits for the outputs that are developed.

An attempt to strengthen collective self-reliance within the Third World should also be complemented by restoring the process of 'massive transfer' through the private banking system to the Third World which, in the 1970s, helped to maintain activity and trade in the world economy and prevented the recession from becoming worse. Its area of operation should be widened to include, for example, the Lomé membership. There is a range of possibilities, extending from relatively modest props to private bank lending to more ambitious schemes involving wider official intervention. I shall now briefly elaborate upon the alternatives currently on the table in order of their degree of ambition.

159

The Role of International Banks

What I have defined as modest proposals have the merit of shoring-up the weaknesses of the private banking system, enabling it to extend the current threshold of lending risk. This approach has the advantage that it can be set up with a minimum of institutional innovation, involving nothing more than a procedure for insuring against those specific risks which threaten to slow down and to halt the pace of lending. Specifically, two classes of risk are involved: (a) project risk, which relates to the inability to repay borrowings from project proceeds, and (b) country risk, which relates to the inability of a country to meet its international payments obligation by virtue of its reserve situation. What has been proposed is an international credit guarantee fund to insure against these two classes of risk, the coverage being limited to commercially viable projects of a minimum size of ten million dollars. The income of this fund would comprise the insurance premia being charged, out of which all claims would normally be met or reserves built up. As a second line of defence, the fund would have determined amounts of paid-in and callable capital. Most importantly, it is capable of being set up on a basis of participation by interested entities – including developed and OPEC countries and institutions such as commercial and investment banks. This proposal was outlined a little while ago by Dr Witteveen, former Managing Director of the International Monetary Fund [*Witteveen, 1980*].

A variant of this scheme, but with a more flexible basis, has crept into the official discussions of the IMF/World Bank Development Committee, i.e. in the work of its Task Force on non-concessional flows. It is intended that a Partial Credit Guarantee Framework of interested countries will be established for the benefit of borrowers known as 'threshold countries', i.e. countries that are not fully creditworthy to lenders on financial terms, without, however, falling into the category of borrowers who would qualify for concessional aid. These partial guarantees would relate to some fraction – less than half – of the loan being sought. Eligibility would require a threshold country to be engaged in an adjustment programme that is

160

acceptable to either the IMF or the World Bank, or to have an adequate appraisal of their economic situation and prospects made by an international financial institution, which is acceptable to the partial credit guarantee framework. In this variant, also, the exclusive project focus of the earlier insurance proposal is relaxed in favour of including programme or sector loans, provided the eligibility criteria are observed.

This range of proposals is addressed more or less explicitly to that category of countries which have hitherto been dependent on the capital markets and are now literally on the threshold of continuing to maintain or of regaining access. Somewhat more ambitious in nature are proposals which seek to tap the guarantee capability of official institutions with a standing in capital markets, to benefit a wider range of countries through subsidising the relending of monies so raised. Two variants can be distinguished here. The first seeks to double World Bank lending by increasing its gearing ratio which at present limits its total lending capability to its total capital. As things stand, when the capital of the World Bank is increased to $80 billion, its lending capability is limited to that amount. The Brandt Commission has proposed to double the Bank's gearing ratio to enable it to lend up to $160 billion. When the Brandt Commission's Report was written it was hoped that the Bank's gearing ratio could be changed without adversely affecting its standing in international capital markets – a matter which requires further consideration in the light of any stringencies that the Bank might currently experience.

Another institution, the European Investment Bank, has already crossed the gearing ratio bridge. The EIB is able to lend up to 250 per cent of its capital which has recently been increased from seven to 14 billion units of account. Its gearing ratio will therefore permit the EIB to lend up to 35 billion European Units of Account (EUA). If outstanding loans of almost EUA 14 million are deducted, the EIB has a lending capability of EUA 21 billion. Its current bond issues have been in the region of EUA three billion per annum. It should be possible, therefore, to use this increased capital base to raise perhaps an additional one billion EUA each year. The amount could be re-lent on substantially concessional terms if amounts currently disbursed by the European Commission to non-ACP countries as grant aid totalling around 200 million EUA, are all diverted to interest subsidy purposes. In other words, use of the EIB's enhanced guarantee capability could convert a modest amount of grant aid into its substantial multiple for purposes of moderately concessional lending. While the magnitudes involved do not imply 'massive transfers', the approach does expand the transfer potential of available budgetary aid amounts.

New Proposals

Still more ambitious proposals have been made which go beyond the notion of a guarantee framework to establishing an explicit large-scale fund for channelling massive transfers for desirable developmental purposes, in particular to fill existing gaps in the present financial structure. These proposals concern the Brandt Commission's World Development Fund, building up to an annual lending programme of $20 billion at the end of a seven year period. In the schedule proposed for this Fund, lending in the seventh year should total $23.5 billion, of which programme lending would represent $18.6 billion and a minimum volume of fuel and non-fuel mineral lending $4.9 billion.

Another, similarly ambitious, massive transfer proposal is that presented by Masaki Nakajima [*1981*], whose proposition for a Global Infrastructure Fund envisages a disbursement programme of a little under $15 billion per annum for the rest of the twentieth century. Taking multiplier effects throughout the world system into account, Nakajima expects his proposal to imply annual expenditures of $25 billion, reaching a cumulative amount of $500 billion by the year 2000. On the same assumption about multiplier effects – roughly twice the initial investment – the Brandt Commission's World Development Fund proposal would imply annual expenditures approaching $50 billion towards the end of its first seven years of operation.

In addition to purely multiplier effects, the two proposals would be expected to create a long-term inducement to invest in those areas of activity which would benefit by the envisaged scale of expenditure. In the case of the World Development Fund this implies those sectors that benefit from programme loan disbursement to developing countries and the energy and mineral sectors. In the Nakajima proposals, on the other hand, expenditures are focused on a range of mega development projects, for example, the greening of the Sahara and major hydroelectric development in India, so as to provide a long-term stimulus for industrial sectors in OECD economies which would supply the necessary inputs. Proposals of this magnitude therefore envisage not only short-term Keynesian multiplier effects but also the long-term application of the Harrodian accelerator principle, under which expected output growth will elicit the desired investments.

Resources for proposals of this scale have to be sought in various ways. The World Development Fund is fairly straight-forward, involving paid-in and callable capital and relying squarely on the international capital market for finance. The Nakajima proposal envisages a division of financing responsibility between OPEC and OECD economies: contributions are expected from government budgets and out of possible savings on disarmament – considerations which, in view of immediate budgetary and political constraints, seem somewhat implausible.

Insofar as capital market stringencies may prejudice World Development Fund-type approaches over the long term, we also have to consider what is perhaps the most ambitious range of proposals for recycling of oil monies. These proposals seek simultaneously to raise resources for massive transfers and to address a central problem which may be expected at best to lead to periodic global macroeconomic uncertainties, and at worst to recessionary shocks to the world economy. This problem is very simply that, in the absence of arrangements for protecting the real value of their financial assets and for effecting an orderly increase in oil prices, OPEC producers are always under pressure to compensate for the gradual erosion in real value of their *stock* of financial assets by introducing sudden and sharp increases in oil prices whenever the market situation warrants it. Indeed, they have every inducement to charge what the traffic will bear in the interests of conserving a non-renewable resource whose value underground, in the absence of negotiated solutions, is likely to be substantially greater tomorrow than its financial equivalent if realised today. Today's softness in the oil market could easily be reversed. In fact, the International

163

Energy Agency has recently argued that such a reversal is highly probable.

The sharp and periodic shifts in world savings resulting from oil price increases inevitably administer deflationary shocks to the world economy. These could be offset, with a lag, by better recycling mechanisms, but the adverse effects on confidence caused by such economic uncertainty will persist.

Proposals to the effect that official arrangements for protecting the real value of OPEC assets should be linked with the long-term financing of developing country deficits through the provision of resources for a World Development Fund, surfaced more or less simultaneously in mid-1980.[3] The Commonwealth Expert Group model, discussed earlier, implies relatively modest protection for OPEC assets against exchange risks only, but places fewer demands on international cooperation in general and on OPEC in particular [*Arndt, 1980: Ch.3; App. 1; Jayawardena, 1980*]. It has the disadvantage, however, of failing to insure against the risk of unilateral price action by OPEC in seeking to offset the erosion in real value of the assets of its members. The Commonwealth proposal proceeds through a series of steps in financial intermediation, summarised as follows:

We strongly recommend that negotiations between interested parties should commence without delay to take the following steps: first, the provision of facilities for reserve diversification by the oil-exporting countries, whether through off-market transactions which would, in effect, create a tier of secondary reserve assets for the participating central banks, or through the proposed IMF Substitution Account; second, the on-lending of such funds via the IMF to developing countries on suitable terms for financing their deficits; and third, consideration of possible ways of making this on-lending process the starting point for long-term programme financing. A feasible mechanism might be the negotiation between governments of appropriate guarantee arrangements. This could later be given permanent form by converting the guarantees into the callable capital (in the sense of a system of limited 'joint and several guarantees') of a lending institution [*Arndt et al., 1980: 84*].

A second proposal, made by Gutowski and Roth, seeks to offer OPEC assets a greater degree of protection by including *additional* measures designed to make the value of oil underground fully equivalent to that of oil converted into financial assets. This involves mutual agreement on a steady annual rate of increase in the real price of oil, and on an equivalent real rate of return on the financial assets – to be denominated in SDRs – into which oil will have been converted. OPEC thus becomes fully protected against both inflation and exchange risks. This greater benefit to OPEC would be in return for explicit long-term assurances of supply and orderly price increases, and therefore makes greater demands on OPEC than do the Commonwealth proposals. The mechanics of the Gutowski-Roth Plan imply offering OPEC each year securities of up to $40 billion, the dollar equivalent of this to be invested in international capital markets. To the extent to which the return on the dollar portfolio falls short of the inflation-indexed return guaranteed to OPEC, there will be a subsidy burden on OECD budgets. An annual fraction of the $40 billion – upwards of $10 billion – is earmarked for a World Development Fund for subsidised lending to developing countries. A third proposal made by the External Relations Committee of the European Parliament seeks in effect to reduce the Gutowski-Roth Plan to a limited sectional initiative on the part of the European Community and the oil-surplus Gulf States. An essential element of all three proposals is the finding of substantial resources for a World Development Fund.

In the current state of the world economy, does any proposal along these lines have a reasonable chance of being negotiated? They all seem to have a degree of inherent political implausibility for the following reasons. First, any attempt to work out a long-term agreement on the price of oil may be thought to detract from the national sovereignty of OPEC countries, and particularly from their freedom to link oil price questions with a wider package involving both international political and economic questions. For this reason difficulties may also arise in implementing the Gutowski-Roth Plan.

The second area of political implausibility relates to the notion of anything that savours of a separate political deal on oil prices and supplies between any part, however significant, of

Lal Jayawardena

OPEC and part of OECD, i.e. the European Community. Pricing decisions require the involvement of *all* OPEC, which is committed to deploying leverage in the area of oil on behalf of the entire Group of 77. The proposed United Nations Global Round would give the opportunity to deploy such leverage in the area of energy – notwithstanding temporary periods of softness in the oil market – in order to negotiate a complex package involving not only financing issues but also, for example, trade and the transfer of technology.

RECOMMENDATIONS FOR THE FUTURE

A basis for forward movement might be provided by an independent initiative to fashion a financial instrument at the level of the European Community, for example, which will provide an attractive medium for the investment of developing country surpluses, and will move towards a link with OECD inflation rates. A SDR-denominated bond would have such an effect, if an appropriate basis could be found for determining a positive real interest rate. In the absence of an accompanying agreement on oil price and supplies, this would not make OPEC completely indifferent as regards oil above ground or oil below ground, but when OECD recovery occurs it could reduce the pressure to restrict supplies and to charge maximum market rates.

In the absence of a parallel agreement with OPEC which would guarantee predictable long-term oil prices, how could such an initiative serve to *safeguard* the future macroeconomic well-being of the world economy? The solution might well consist in timing the introduction in sufficient volume of an inflation-indexed asset at a moment of appropriate 'softness' in the oil market. One way of ensuring the desired predictability would be to couple that introduction with an indication of the minimum amounts likely to be offered annually for, say, a five-year period, and an announcement that the annual offer will *lapse* if at any time the real price of oil were to increase by more than a specific annual percentage above that of a base line period.

An alternative formula for introducing the inflation-indexed asset would be to set it up as a bond whose real rate of return would vary inversely with the real price of oil, perhaps with a provision that a *negative* real rate of return would automatically attach to past annual issues of the bond should the real price of oil increase beyond a specific annual percentage. If the annual volume of assets on offer is sufficiently *large* in relation to other stock holdings of OPEC surplus countries which perhaps yield indifferent and uncertain real returns, this formula would offer a powerful inducement to shift that stock into the new asset, as well as to maintain the price of oil on an even course. Since the shifts in the OPEC assets portfolio would be purely voluntary, in response to the incentives and disincentives built into the package offered by the Community, the details would need to be worked out with considerable care, on the basis of informed consultation with OPEC portfolio managers. OPEC would be offered a steady long-term rate of return on a financial asset which would be immune to fluctuation, in the hope that the desired predictability of oil price rises would emerge as a consequence. This proposal has the further advantage of enabling the institution that will administer the scheme to invest its counterpart dollars in joint ventures in the Third World, thereby *complementing* current proposals for setting-up a southern financial institution for promoting such ventures.

If Europe were to be generous in a spirit of enlightened self-interest, it might wish further to demarcate some minimum portion of this offer in SDRs, thereby guaranteeing against exchange risks, on condition that OPEC would convert oil price increases beyond a base line price into loans of varying concessionality for oil-importing LDCs. In this way, it will be recalled, OPEC sought to give grants or interest-free long-term loans to countries with less than $300 per capita income which import less than 10,000 barrels of oil a day; concessional long-term loans with a 25 to 50 per cent grant element to countries with per capita incomes of between $300 and $1000 and oil imports of between 10,000 and 100,000 barrels a day; and medium-term commercial loans to countries with per capita incomes of more than $1000 and oil imports of more than 100,000 barrels a day. The minimum volume of exchange risk-proof securities offered by the Community could be equated to the concessional financing burden assumed in this way by OPEC. The effect would be to maintain Third World purchasing power and creditworthiness, thus benefiting the

Community, while offering OPEC a significant measure of protection.

Implementation of this aspect of OPEC's long-term strategy could be coupled with a more imaginative approach to conditionality than has characterised the traditional approaches of the Bretton Woods Institutions. OPEC's restoration of the equivalent of oil price increases beyond a base line price to oil importing LDCs could be tantamount to enforcement of an equivalent degree of 'forced savings'. The conditions under which this could occur might imply earmarking domestic currency counterparts of the sums being restituted for desirable developmental objectives, including structural adjustment programmes. This is a familiar extension of current OPEC Fund, World Bank and IMF practice, and could be combined with the conditions underlying a supplementary financing scheme. But the objectives of the institution managing the plan would be strengthened if at least some local currencies were to become part of the domestic equity of triangular joint ventures involving oil-importing LDCs, OPEC and the Community.

If the two classes of security specified above were to be offered through an institution of the kind contemplated in the Gutowski-Roth Plan, the problem would be to assure its solvency. This problem would arise if the institution's liabilities in respect of interest payments were to exceed the return on its portfolio assets, acquired by investing the dollars with which OPEC countries will have paid for their protected securities. Discussion of the Gutowski-Roth Plan has been further complicated by the prospect of any such excess becoming a subsidy burden on OECD governments. If, however, the institution were authorised to invest its dollars in *equities* which hedge against inflation, in addition to other instruments, the institution's viability could be ensured at the cost of some sacrifice in the ease with which OPEC could convert 'protected' securities into cash. A more detailed formulation of this proposal would ensure the institution's financial viability, and a balance between protection of value and the liquidity of securities issued to OPEC, leaving developed country governments with a subsidy burden which is imputable solely to the cost of lending under the World Development Fund (WDF) component of the proposal. Under appropriate circumstances,

SDR creation could finance any such subsidy amount without burdening government budgets.

If, as envisaged, the centerpiece of the plan would involve OPEC portfolio diversification on a joint venture basis into real capital formation in the Third World, and if, as part of the conditionality inherent in the exercise, part of the LDC equity stake is linked to restitution of increments in the oil price above a baseline level, then the only politically viable basis on which to proceed would be an institutional structure which would give oil-importing LDCs and OPEC members a vital stake in the overall management of the equity funds.

Any framework for promoting joint ventures in the Third World would require at least the following elements:

(a) a political risk guarantee;

(b) a 'pool of commercial risks' covering only part of the investments (to be determined for each programme); this could very well take the form of the institution in question implementing the Witteveen proposal for providing insurance cover for project loans of a minimum size;

(c) performance rules for foreign investors supplying know-how and for recipient countries. The purpose of these rules would be to reduce risks to the competitiveness of the projects, as well as to bring about the desired long run transfer of technology to developing countries.

If these rules for the management of equity investments were to be incorporated into the structure of the institution envisaged, their acceptance would proceed on a purely voluntary basis. Developing countries that opt for these arrangements could expect to benefit from equity funds available to the institution. If the Southern Financing Institution for joint ventures already mentioned were to materialise, it could function as a leading merchant bank for promoting joint ventures. Any investment whose legitimacy was established by token equity participation of a Southern investment institution, could *a fortiori* attract equity funds from the wider institution envisaged for administering the inflation-indexed bond proposal. Alternatively, as the Southern institution expands its participation in joint ventures, this could in time be acquired by the *wider* institution as part of its own equity portfolio.[4]

SUMMARY AND CONCLUSIONS

It may be worthwhile to recapitulate the proposal developed above as follows. World recovery is impeded by the growing incapacity of the private banking system to continue to on-lend surpluses, wherever they occur, to developing and other countries in the manner in which recycling was accomplished after the first oil price increases. OPEC surpluses no longer exist and the Japanese and German surpluses which have replaced them confront a weakened banking system. The need is therefore for a catalyst to set in motion a process of recovery.

This catalyst might well consist of the opportunity created in the proposal for portfolio diversification of OPEC assets currently held in the financial markets of industrial countries and Eurocurrency markets – a total of 400 billion dollars. Of this stock, a significant proportion may be annually shiftable into real capital formation in the South, provided the necessary framework for project development and protection against risk is assured for the private parties and private banks necessarily involved.

It is the feedback on developed economies of the payment for capital goods so generated which can initiate a virtuous circle of recovery. It is also an underlying premise that the institutions in which OPEC assets are currently parked are less able to on-lend the counterpart dollars for the purpose of real capital formation.

Against this background, the plan involves a balanced package requiring the adaptation of the Gutowski-Roth plan to a soft oil market situation. An indexed asset into which current OPEC portfolios could be diversified would be offered, for example by the European Community, under conditions which would simultaneously encourage predictability and gradualness in the oil price, thereby insulating the world's macroeconomic management from random shocks. The dollar counterpart of the assets being issued would be invested in a range of equities, including investments in the Third World, whose returns would ensure the solvency of the institution handling the indexed asset issues and simultaneously promote a process of real capital formation in the South. The details can best be described in terms of the obligations of the various parties to the arrangement, namely, of the European Community which would be offering the asset, the institution which would be administering the asset, and of OPEC.

The Community's Obligations

(a) The Community would meet any interest subsidy cost on that portion of the assets of the institution administering the plan which is devoted to lending to developing countries. (b) It would make a minimum issue of exchange risk-protected securities equivalent to the estimated annual volume of concessional financing granted by OPEC to developing countries to meet price increases above the base line oil price. (c) It would make a supplementary issue of both exchange risk and inflation risk-protected securities which would *lapse* if the real price of oil should increase annually by a fixed percentage above the base line price; this could be reinforced by arrangements whereby the real rate of return on an asset would vary inversely with the real price of oil. (d) It would keep institution building to a minimum by issuing the protected securities through a European Investment Bank window.

The Institution's Obligations

(a) The institution's asset portfolio would be distributed between equities and other assets in such a manner as to ensure an acceptable combination of protection of value and liquidity of the counterpart securities for OPEC so that the fund becomes viable except for the subsidy component of WDF lending; the limits to OPEC illiquidity ought to be capable of advance specification. It would also incorporate an umbrella for the management of triangular joint ventures on the basis of rules that are acceptable to interested countries, involving joint management by developed, developing and OPEC participants.

OPEC's Obligations

(a) OPEC would implement for developing countries the proposals contained in its long-term strategy for concessional financing of oil imports, possibly linked to structural adjustment programmes and to building-up local currency counter-

171

part funds for investment inequities. (b) It would 'accept' restrictions on encashing protected securities if the financial viability of the institution is to be preserved without a subsidy on Community budgets other than the amount required to subsidise WDF lending; no prior agreement needs to be reached because 'absorption' of the securities will depend on the balance provided between protection of real value and liquidity; there would be substantial scope for varying this balance and the amount offered so as to equate supply and demand for the securities.

Adaptation of the Gutowski-Roth Plan would enable the Community to take a bold initiative in the context of a 'soft' oil market, without entering into excessively complex negotiations and exposing it to unpredictable financial risks. It would benefit OPEC, the developing countries, and above all, the European Community itself. The relevance of such an initiative is reinforced by the views of the President of OPEC, Eduardo Ortega Gomez, then Ecuador's Oil Minister:

> The Organisation of Petroleum Exporting Countries (OPEC) has defeated the industrialised countries which wanted to give it a hammering by building up large oil stocks to weaken the oil cartel's hold over prices. In the wake of this defeat a climate of opinion is emerging which could produce a period of long-term oil price stability through a new relationship between OPEC and the oil consumers.

In this context, Ortega stresses the need for stability in oil prices: 'The need for stability in oil prices was not appreciated before. Now everyone accepts this as important.'

The report continues:

> Ortega was pleased to note that Japan's Trade Minister had undertaken to raise the subject of a new relationship with OPEC among fellow Organisation for Economic Cooperation and Development (OECD) members. OPEC in turn will now be pushing its long delayed discussions on long-term strategy to the top of the agenda. When, in 1978, Saudi Arabia first proposed that the cartel should find a new and more stable way of fixing oil prices, it ran into opposition from a vocal minority of OPEC members. Ortega now be-

lieves that the recent experience of falling rather than rising prices has made all his fellow members keen to go ahead. [Cf *Vines, 1982*].

Against this background of views published on OPEC's behalf, is it too much to expect an initiative from the European Community towards the South as a whole in an area in which the mutuality of interests between the various groupings in the world community are perhaps the most pronounced?

NOTES

1. See Jayawardena [*1978*], for a survey of the evidence concerning the disposition of slack capacities in Europe and possible structural mismatches. The discussion below draws on this paper as well as on Jayawardena [*1981*].

2. G24 stands for the Group of 24 developing countries which have prepared proposals for reform of the IMF.

3. See Arndt [*1980*], Ch. 3: 'The Balance of Payments Problem', and Appendix 1: 'Joint Guarantees and the Evolution of the World Development Fund: A Scheme'. Also, Gutowski & Roth [*1980*], and European Parliament Committee on External Economic Relations [*1980*].

4. The sketch for the triangular umbrella described above draws heavily upon a comment made by Monsieur A. L. Dangeard of the Bureau de Recherches Géologiques et Minières, Paris, to whom I am most grateful. M. Dangeard has suggested that a start be made in areas where there is a current international momentum – for example, energy development and food production.

REFERENCES

Arndt, H. et al., 1980, *The World Economic Crisis: A Commonwealth Perspective*, A Report of a Group of Experts, London, Commonwealth Secretariat.
Commission of the European Communities (CEC), 1979, *Europe and the Third World. A Study on Interdependence*, Brussels, EEC.
European Commission, 1981, *European Report No. 761*.
European Parliament Committee on External Economic Relations, 1980, *Draft Report on Trade Relations Between the EEC and the Gulf States*.
Gutowski, A., & W. Roth, 1980, *Draft of a Contractual Agreement Between OPEC Countries, Industrial Countries and Developing Countries*, Hamburg.
Holsen, J. A. & J. L. Waelbroeck, 1976, 'The Less Developed Countries and the International Monetary Mechanism', *Papers and Proceedings of the 88th Annual Meeting of the American Economic Association, American Economic Review*, May, 171-76.

IBIDI, 1981, *The Brandt Commission Papers*, Geneva.

IMF, 1982, *World Economic Outlook*, Washington.

Jayawardena, L., 1978, 'The Third World as an Engine of World Growth', Presidential Address to the Sri Lanka Association for the Advancement of Science, Colombo.

Jayawardena, L., 1980, 'The Massive Transfer of Resources to Developing Countries', a paper submitted to the Commonwealth Group of Experts, and also to the International Banking Conference, Dubrovnik.

Jayawardena, L., 1981, 'The Oil Price and the Balance of Payments', address to a seminar on the Brandt Commission Report convened by the Friedrich Ebert Foundation, Brussels.

Jayawardena, L., 1982, 'Plenary Statement as Leader of the Sri Lanka Delegation to the South/South Consultations', New Delhi.

Jenkins, The Right Hon. R., 1977, 'Europe's Present Challenge and Future Opportunity', Jean Monnet Lecture, Florence.

Morgan Guaranty Trust, 1980, *World Financial Markets*, New York.

Nakajima, M., 1978, *A Proposition for the 'Global Infrastructure Fund'*, Tokyo.

UNCTAD, 1979, *Arusha Programme for Collective Self-Reliance and Framework for Negotiations*, Manila.

UNCTAD, 1981, *Trade and Development Report*, New York.

Vines, S., 1982, 'Ortega Oils OPEC's Troubled Waters', *London Observer*, 30 May.

Witteveen, H. J., 1980, 'Outlook for Investment Banking', Address to a *Financial Times* Conference, Colombo.

X

Monetarist Policies on a World Scale

by JACQUES POLAK

THE WORLD ECONOMY, THE INTERNATIONAL MONETARY SYSTEM, MONETARIST POLICIES – CAUSE AND EFFECT

There can be no question that the performance of the world economy in the 1970s and the early 1980s has been much less satisfactory than in the first quarter of a century after the end of World War II. Growth has been much lower, productivity has become nearly flat, and unemployment and inflation are much higher; the contrast in experience between the two periods is too striking, and too familiar to all of us, to require proof by citing strings of numbers. There is, moreover, ever-increasing evidence that the process of liberalisation of trade, one of the most welcome features of the 1950s and 1960s, is grinding to a halt if not shifting into reverse.

At about the same time that this sharp change occurred in the economic climate – let us say in the early 1970s – equally striking changes took place in the world's financial policies. Much of the change in the world financial structure occurred without much planning, more by the forces of economic nature than by conscious international decision making. Thus, the par value system, introduced in 1946, broke down in 1971-73 and was replaced by a de facto regime of floating exchange rates for the major currencies. The fixed price of gold in terms of the dollar (and, via fixed exchange rates, in terms of other currencies as well) was abandoned when it proved untenable. The

175

value of gold reserves increased ten to twentyfold, but by the same token gold became too speculative an asset to be used any longer for settlements among central banks. The world thus landed in an almost pure dollar standard which then gradually transformed itself into a multi-currency reserve system as additional currencies (the DM, the Yen, the Swiss franc) gained reserve status. Commercial banks – their deposits swollen by the proceeds of oil exports at greatly increased prices – rediscovered the attractions of foreign lending and, after a few years' lag, are also rediscovering the risks of foreign lending. Amidst all these happenings, there was of course the deliberate decision to introduce into the system the Special Drawing Right (SDR) of the International Monetary Fund. In spite of major efforts, however, the role of the SDR has remained small and it has not had any important effect on the workings of the system.

On the policy side, many governments have learned the limitations of controlling (let alone fine-tuning) their economies by Keynesian-type demand management policies and have put increasing emphasis on monetary or monetarist approaches.

We have thus, on the one hand, highly unsatisfactory developments in the world economy and, on the other hand and roughly coincidentally, important changes in the international financial structure and in national financial policies. What are we to make out of these two observations? *Is there a causal connection between them, and if so, in which direction does it run?* This is the central issue that I shall discuss because it obviously needs to be answered if we are to know in which direction we should look for solutions or remedies. In accordance with the general theme of this book, I shall pay particular attention to the developing countries; but I leave it to other contributors to discuss how monetary management can assist the LDCs when they face problems of balance of payments adjustment. I developed the theoretical framework for this 25 years ago [*Polak, 1957*]. My policy view on the matter is that monetary management is a necessary but not a sufficient condition to bring about adjustment; in most instances, it will need to be complemented by what may be called 'structural policies'.

In our search for causal connections, we have to pose questions such as the following. Are the present economic difficulties – in the developed world and in the Third World – in some sense attributable to changes in the system and changes in policy? Could we make our way back to 'the good old days' by returning to past features of the system and to the policy approaches of those days? Or are the changes in the system, and the adoption of different policies to those of the 1950s and 1960s, the necessary results of the development of the world economy, so that our only way out of the present morass is forward, not backward? I shall address this question first, briefly and without detailed argumentation, with respect to the international monetary system and then, at somewhat greater length, with respect to domestic policies in the industrial countries. Thereafter, I shall discuss the scope that I see for measures to relieve the pressure on developing countries.

THE INTERNATIONAL MONETARY SYSTEM

Many would probably share the view of the Brandt Commission [*1980: 205*-7] that the 'current monetary disorder' is an important cause of present difficulties and that, for that reason, 'reform of the world monetary system is urgent' with respect to 'the exchange rate regime, the reserve system ... and the adjustment mechanism.' The Commission recommended that this reform should build on 'the large measure of consensus which emerged in the Committee of Twenty' [*Ibidem: 219*] (the Ministerial Committee of the IMF which studied monetary reform from 1972 to 1974).

In my view, this approach to the current situation of the world economy does not hold much promise of success. It fails to recognise the fact that, at least in most of its features, the present system was the result – I should stress, the unwanted result, because it was accepted with great reluctance by almost all official participants – of very strong forces working toward the destruction of the previous (pre-1971) system. It is also a mistaken reading of history to assume that there existed, about a decade ago, a broad consensus on reform which, for some unfortunate reason, countries then failed to put into effect. The fact is that on certain fundamental points, such as the exchange rate system and the provisions for the settlement of balance of payments surpluses and deficits, there was no agreement among the major countries; and there would be even less general support now than there was then for many of the proposals made in the Committee of Twenty.[1]

DOMESTIC POLICIES OF THE INDUSTRIAL COUNTRIES

In the late 1960s and early 1970s, policy in most industrial countries could be described as striking a delicate balance between the rate of growth and the inflation rate. Countries could be seen as opting for different combinations of these two variables which were supposed to be connected by a 'Phillips curve'. In practice, however, the countries tended to shade policy risks on the side of growth and employment, and without adequate attention to inflationary side effects [*IMF, 1976: 12*]. They thus ended up with more inflation, and especially more intractable inflationary expectations, than they had bargained for.

The harmful effects of inflation became increasingly evident. In many countries, the management of existing assets became a far more profitable activity than the management of production. The rise in productivity which for two or three decades had permitted rising real wages, evaporated, but real wages continued to rise nevertheless. Government expenditure increased sharply everywhere, leading to large deficits even as the share of GDP taken by taxation rose. In a number of European countries, the share of wages in total output became excessive, profitability declined, investment became unattractive and the demand for labour declined.

It was this general experience which gradually caused countries to change the direction of their economic policies towards recognition of the need to bring inflation under control as a precondition for sustained growth. This change in policy could be considered to have been completed by the time of the Fund's 1979 Annual Meeting, when the so-called Interim Committee, which represents the whole of the Fund's membership, denounced inflation in more specific terms than it had ever done before:

The Committee observed with great concern that inflation

throughout the industrial world had intensified. In view of this grave threat to economic and financial stability, the Committee emphasized that the main task of economic policy was to contain inflationary pressures and to reduce inflationary expectations. One of the immediate problems was to prevent the recent surge of price increases for oil and other primary products from adding to the strength of inflationary expectations and thus being built into underlying rates of increase in wages and prices. Accordingly, the Committee noted with satisfaction that reduction of inflation was being given priority in the economic policies of industrial countries, and it reiterated its view [first expressed in March 1979] that in many countries progress in reducing inflation was an essential precondition for the resumption of vigorous growth.[2]

The instruments by which these new policy objectives were to be pursued differed from country to country, but monetary policy played a large role in many countries. Not that monetary policy had previously been idle: indeed it had been employed a great deal – 'flexibly' as the term of praise went at the time – in the attempt to fine-tune economies along the narrow path of near-full employment. The likely degree of success of attempts at short-term management of the economy by means of variations in monetary policy is open to question, however, among other things because the effects of changes in monetary policy on aggregate demand occur with a substantial lag. The chances are much better if the policy objective is to steer the economy on as steady an average course as possible by controlling the growth rate of the money supply. This objective has in recent years been adopted in a number of major industrial countries. It is subject to a host of technical problems, which need not concern us here. But in principle, and to a considerable extent in practice as well, it is possible to bring about a target growth rate of nominal GNP by controlling the rate of growth in a suitably defined version of the money supply. Monetary policy cannot (indeed, and more generally: demand management cannot) determine how the growth of nominal GNP will be divided between real growth and inflation. In some countries and in some circumstances, it may

179

be possible to use incomes policies to reduce the inflation component; otherwise the same objective will be achieved, probably more slowly, by the working of the monetary policy itself.

Allow me to elaborate on this point with the aid of figures drawn from the experience of the United States since it adopted a predominantly monetarist approach in late 1979. The figures in Table 1 refer to percentage changes in the three years 1980 to 1982. For the first two years, the figures are actual; for 1982, the figure for the growth in the money supply is the upper part of the target range of the Federal Reserve Board, and the other figures are Federal Reserve forecasts. In round figures both the growth in the money supply, measured here as M_2, and the growth in nominal GNP lie in the range of nine to ten per cent per year in each of the three years. But there is a gradual shift in the two components of money GNP: the inflation figures decline from ten to nine to an expected seven per cent, and real growth rises from slightly negative in 1980 to about one per cent in 1981 and to an expected central value of near two per cent in 1982.

It should be added that the functioning of the monetary process would not normally be expected to show up in such simple and convincing numbers; but even if this example may be almost too good to be true, it is appropriate to illustrate the model that I want to bring to your attention.

If monetary policy is relied upon to determine aggregate demand, decisions on the level of government expenditure will determine the distribution of demand between the government and the private sector, and the fiscal deficit will importantly affect the level of interest rates. It is through high interest rates that a large budget deficit crowds out private expenditure on new equipment, house building, and consumer durables within a given growth rate of aggregate demand. Thus, the impact of severe pressure against the monetary ceiling in one country will be felt by other countries in the rise in interest rates, which in turn can have a sharp impact on exchange rates. For the developing countries, which are debtors on a large scale with much of the debt at floating interest rates, the main impact arises via high interest rates. This will have an immediate and large negative effect. Every one percentage point increase in

TABLE 1

Money Supply and GNP in the United States
(percentage changes)

(4th quarter of year over 4th quarter of preceding year)

	1980	1981	1982*
1. M_2	9.2	9.5	8.9[a]
2. Increase in Velocity	0.2	0.3	0.5
3. Nominal GNP	9.4	9.8	9.0
4. Inflation	9.8	8.9	7.0[b]
5. Real Growth	−0.3	0.9	2.0[b]

Source: Federal Reserve Board

*Forecast as of February 1982.
[a]Upper part of the range.
[b]Approximate middle of the range (6½ to 7¾ for line 4, 1½ to 3 for line 5).

Notes: Line 2: Line 3 − Line 1.
Line 3: Line 4 + Line 5.
Line 4: GNP deflator.
Line 5: GNP at 1972 prices.

Eurodollar rates adds two billion US dollars to the annual debt service of the non-oil developing countries. Note that there is no presumption that strict control over the money supply by itself produces high interest rates. Switzerland has long combined a strict monetary policy aimed at a low inflation rate with the lowest interest rates in the world. In the United States, the approach to controlling inflation by means of monetary policy was bound to raise interest rates in the short term, but the persistence of high interest rates in that country is to be attributed to present and expected large government deficits.

As I have indicated, the basic policy attitude of most of the industrial countries is to focus their attention primarily on combatting inflation and to accept the relatively slow growth that this approach implies for the near future. For the developing countries, this policy amounts to a slowdown in the demand for their export products (which is affecting both

181

quantities and prices), offset to some extent by a reduction in the inflation rate for the products that these countries import from the industrial countries and, as we have seen in recent months, a decline in the price of oil. The industrial countries evidently (and, I believe, correctly) consider that the hardship that they impose on themselves by the pursuit of this policy approach is, on balance, justified by the absolute need to combat inflationary expectations as a precondition for the resumption of sustained growth. These policies also impose hardships on the developing countries. Not, probably, greater hardships than those that would result from inability of the industrial countries to bring inflation under control, i.e. from a permanent state of stagflation in the world economy. But without question, there are hardships in the short run. This poses the need to consider policy options which will minimise the immediate negative impact on the developing countries. Before discussing these options we should stress the imperative need not to increase the burden on these countries by the introduction of protectionist measures against their exports.

MEASURES TO ALLEVIATE THE POSITION OF THE DEVELOPING COUNTRIES

Policy Action to Reduce Interest Rates

The first measure, already mentioned, is recognition of the need to adjust fiscal policy in developed countries to the constraints of monetary policy. There is no reason to assume that the conflict between the two arms of policy serves the interests of any country, and international pressure is clearly called for to reinforce national pressure to remove this conflict. What is needed is not (as it is sometimes called) a different 'policy mix': stricter fiscal policy and a loosening of monetary policy. The need is rather for recognition that government deficits – in many industrial countries – need to be cut because they absorb an excessive proportion of available savings and thereby pre-empt resources from investment, both in the industrial world and in developing countries. If fewer resources are taken, net, by government, the same monetary policy will produce lower interest rates, thereby encouraging investment.

Safeguarding the Recycling Mechanism

Second, the conditions that have permitted the developing world to continue to grow at a fairly satisfactory pace while the industrial world has become mired in stagflation, should be safeguarded. The differential in growth rates is, of course, a most notable development in itself, and one not readily expected by those who see the industrial countries as the sole motor of the world economy (Table 2).

TABLE 2

Average Annual Growth Rates (per cent)

	1968-72	1972-77	1978-81
Industrial countries	4.4	3.0	2.5
Net oil importing developing countries*	5.8	5.2	3.8
Major exporters of manufactures	8.1	6.2	3.8
Low-income countries*	3.4	3.9	3.4
Other net oil importers	5.5	4.8	3.9

*Excluding People's Republic of China.
Source: IMF, *World Economic Outlook*, various.

An essential precondition for the persistence of the differential in growth rates in favour of developing countries is the safeguarding of the flow of private capital to these countries. This flow has developed in response to the high savings rates in a number of oil-exporting countries with relatively small absorptive capacities, through the recycling mechanism provided by the banks in the industrial countries. The magnitude of these flows will need to be adjusted to the reduction in oil surpluses and to the change in economic outlook for most developing countries. But it is important that these flows continue to provide a major source of capital. This will require, first, policies by the receiving countries to maintain their creditworthiness. It also requires the conduct by the banks of their overseas lending business in such a manner as to avoid, to the largest extent possible, crisis situations in individual countries.

And, lastly, it requires that the financial authorities in the banks' home countries assist the banks in prudential management and stand ready, in an emergency, to protect the functioning of the system.[3] While the first of these three requirements is the responsibility of individual developing countries, the latter two have to be met in the industrial world.

The arrangements in industrial countries need to be backed up by a strong International Monetary Fund. The Fund must be able to assist, sometimes on a very large scale, individual countries that may find themselves in intractable payments positions and which are prepared to take the adjustment measures required. And the Fund must also be ready to support the solidity of the system, for example against the risk that important links in the mechanism of recycling may break down under pressure.

Resumption of Allocations of SDRs

There is a further, if only a modest, contribution that the Fund can make to the debt problem of developing countries, and of many other countries as well. The developing countries, like others, feel the need for a trend increase in the level of their foreign exchange reserves, broadly in line with the secular rise in the value of their international transactions. The amount involved is substantial: over the past decade, the reserves of LDCs increased on average by an amount of SDR five billion a year. Acquisition of these amounts of reserves through the market mechanism involved, directly or indirectly, an increase in foreign borrowing and hence – even if this borrowing could be arranged without difficulty – the use of some portion of these countries' access to credit, which is by no means unlimited. To the extent that the Fund meets the needs of its members for increases in reserves through the annual allocation of SDRs, countries can preserve their access to credit and, incidentally, also acquire reserves at a somewhat lower interest cost.

Enlarged and Improved Aid Flows

In contrast to SDR allocations, which are made to all members of the Fund in proportion to their quotas, the maintenance of the flow of private capital to the developing world does not benefit equally the different groups of countries in that world. These flows are of primary interest to the newly industrial countries, i.e. the developing countries that are major exporters of manufactures. These countries have already been the most successful of the developing countries in terms of growth rates (Table 2). Action with respect to capital flows must therefore be complemented by policies to raise official development assistance and – once one recognises the limited measure of success that this recommendation is unfortunately likely to meet – by measures to channel available aid in the first place toward low-income developing countries.

I have mentioned a number of policy fields in which action could be taken to alleviate the pressure that the present world economic situation exercises on developing countries. I do not want to imply that advocacy of these policies will ensure their adoption, nor even that their adoption will bring great relief to the developing countries. To a major extent these countries find themselves in one boat with the industrial countries, sharing together prosperity (past prosperity, as well as, one may hope, future prosperity) but also sharing adversity.

WHERE NOT TO LOOK FOR SOLUTIONS

I turn now to the discussion of certain approaches which, while designed to relieve the present economic situation of developing countries, in my opinion do not hold promise of achieving their intended objective.

The first of these would be to call off monetarism in the industrial world. For the reasons that I have already set out, I believe this approach to be mistaken. Monetarism in this context stands for the containment of demand, and the industrial countries are pursuing containment of demand for an important purpose: to bring inflation under control. In the last two years, the policy has achieved important results in many of the industrial countries. Control over monetary variables is not conducted perfectly in any country, and it needs support from other policies, as I have discussed. The policy implies costs at home, which are endured because of expected long-run benefits; it is unreasonable to suggest that it be abandoned on

185

the ground that it also has costs abroad, just when it is showing an important measure of success.

A second approach that I believe to be doomed to failure is that which appears under the caption of 'International Keynesianism'. A certain measure of support for this approach can be inferred from the section in the Brandt Report [*1980: 241*] which deals with 'The Need for "Massive Transfers"'. A wide variety of possible measures are discussed in this section, and also in Jayawardena's contribution to this book, many of which I would endorse; but I am referring here to the suggestion for 'pump-priming of the world economy, which would help it out of recession in the short term, and contribute to higher growth in the longer run' [*Ibidem: 67*]. I can see no place for international pump-priming, or international deficit financing, in a world where the internationally adopted policy stance – as reflected in the communiqué of the Interim Committee that I cited earlier – points in the opposite direction. One might well ask: 'Why should Northern governments, hesitant to stimulate their own economies in a period of stagflation, find more virtue in a process of stimulation which operates via the developing countries?' That question is found in the Brandt Report [*Ibidem: 67-68*] and it is not really answered.

The call for 'International Keynesianism' strikes me as a curious throwback to a body of economic theory from the early decades of this century: the theory of economic imperialism associated with Rosa Luxemburg [*1913*] and other Marxist writers, which held that crises in the capitalist world could only be overcome by injections of demand from the less developed world, financed by capital flows to these countries. We no longer live in this pre-Keynesian world. We have experimented with the Keynesian recipes and we have learned their merits *and* their limitations. If the industrial countries do not adopt reflationary economic politics, it is not because they do not know how to do this, but because they have reached a deliberate decision that Keynesian remedies are not the answer to the present situation. If ever they come to a different view on the needs of the situation – for example because inflation has been brought under control – they will certainly find it more expeditious to reflate their own economies than to reach international agreement on a programme of reflation which would start in the developing world. In that situation the domestic approach in the industrial countries would be the most beneficial for all concerned, including the developing countries. Any other approach would be far less effective, either in terms of speed of action or of the amounts that could be marshalled.

CONCLUDING REMARKS

The rapid and easy expansion of the world economy during the first quarter of a century after World War II has ill-prepared us for the difficulties that we are now facing. It has gradually become clear that the remedies applied to overcome slight dips during that period of sustained expansion are not suitable for the present problems of persistent stagflation; they bear, indeed, some of the responsibility for bringing this condition into existence. I have tried to survey the role that the monetary (or the 'monetarist') approach can play in this new situation, using the monetarist label as a short-cut expression to refer to the constraint on aggregate demand, which – as I have made clear – needs the support of an appropriate fiscal policy and often of a variety of other policies as well. Unlike the earlier remedies, the medicine sold under the monetarist label is neither quick-acting nor painless. And, as if this were not enough bad news, its success cannot be guaranteed, precisely because monetary measures take time and impose hardships. Success will materialise only if the policy is persevered in until its aim, the control over inflation, has been solidly achieved. Successive temporary bouts of constraint, interspersed with periods of relaxation, are worse than useless; they impose hardships without producing anything to show for them.

I am aware that this is not a particularly cheerful note to conclude on. Naturally, the widespread nostalgia for the 'good old days', to which I referred earlier, extends also to the policy prescriptions of these days. Unfortunately, in the situation in which we find ourselves now, they don't work.

NOTES

1. For a good discussion of the areas of disagreement, and of the various national positions, see Williamson [*1977*].

2. Interim Committee of the Board of Governors on the International Monetary System, Press Communiqué, Belgrade, 1 October 1979 [*IMF, 1980: 152*].

3. These various aspects are discussed in Group of Thirty [*1981*].

REFERENCES

Brandt Commission Report, 1980, *North-South: A Programme for Survival.* The Report of the Independent Commission on International Development Issues under the Chairmanship of Willy Brandt; Cambridge, Mass., MIT Press, and London, Pan Books Ltd.
Group of Thirty, 1981, *Balance of Payments Problems of Developing Countries,* New York.
IMF, 1976, *Annual Report,* Washington, DC.
IMF, 1977, *The Monetary Approach to the Balance of Payments,* Washington, DC.
IMF, 1980, *Annual Report,* Washington, DC.
IMF, *World Economic Outlook,* Washington, DC.
Luxemburg, R., 1968, *The Accumulation of Capital,* New York, Monthly Review Press (first published in German in 1913).
Polak, J.J., 1957, 'Monetary Analysis of Income Formation and Payments Problems', IMF Staff Papers; reprinted in IMF, 1977.
Williamson, J., 1977, *The Failure of Monetary Reform 1970-1974,* Sunbury on Thames, Thomas Nelson & Sons Ltd.

Index

aid (Official Development
  Assistance), 114, 121, 129,
  132, 146, 151, 155, 156, 158,
  160, 161, 184, 185
Algeria, 12, 158
Allende (Government), 53, 116,
  117, 125n
Argentina, 39n, 111, 112, 113, 116,
  119, 120, 121, 123
Arndt, H., 154, 164, 173n
Arusha Meeting (Arusha
  Programme of Group of 77),
  151, 152

Baer, W., 124n
balance of payments
  problems (crisis), 2, 19, 22,
    23, 24, 32, 37, 62, 63, 64,
    66, 67, 85, 105, 112, 123,
    128, 131, 134, 135, 145, 176
  current account deficit, 10-15,
    17, 19, 23, 36, 154, 155
  foreign exchange shortage
    (constraint), 22, 112, 113,
    118, 128, 141
Balassa, B., 33, 34, 40n
Bangladesh, 39n
Bank of International Settlements
  (BIS), 23, 39n, 40n, 41n
Barre (Barre Government), 62
Barsony, A., 34, 40n
Belgium, 80, 81, 86, 88
Benoist, A. de, 94n
Berg Report, 128, 142

Billip, M., 94n
Birman, I., 99
Bismarck, 87
Bolivia, 39n
Bosworth, B. P. 124n
Brandt Commission, 152, 156, 161,
  162, 177, 186
Brazil, 12, 39n, 40n, 80, 111, 112,
  114, 116, 118, 119, 121, 125n
Bretton Woods (Bretton Woods
  System), 10, 16, 45, 46, 52,
  65, 84, 85, 127, 168
Brooks, J., 54n
budget deficit (see under Fiscal
  Policy)
Bulgaria, 98
Bush, G., 49

Castro, F., 125n
Cambridge Department of Applied
  Economics, 79
Cambridge Economic Policy Group,
  41n
Central Bank (see monetary
  authorities)
Central Intelligence Agency (CIA),
  116
centrally planned economies (State
  Socialist Economies), 2, 3, 5,
  12, 20, 25, 96-109
  Council for Mutual Economic
    Assistance (CMEA), 105, 106
CEPAL (see Economic Commission
  for Latin America),

189

Index

Chile, 40n, 53, 54, 89, 111, 112, 116, 117, 118, 119, 120, 121, 123

China, People's Republic of, 20, 39n, 105, 106

coinage, history of, 43-44

Colombia, 111

Commonwealth Group of Experts, 154, 158, 164, 165

Congo, 39n

Cripps, F., 3, 10, 17, 21, 26, 38, 40n, 41n

Crockett, A. D., 33

crowding out, 21, 100, 180

Cuba, 98, 99, 121, 125n

current account deficit (see under balance of payments)

Czechoslovakia, 98, 118

DAC Report, 128

Dangeard, A. L., 173n

Davidson P., 103

debt,
external, 2, 7, 12, 14, 15, 17, 18, 19, 25, 35, 65, 81, 157, 180
servicing, 12, 15, 31, 38, 181

Denmark, 81

DDR (see Germany, Dem. Rep.)

devaluation (see Exchange Rate)

development planning, 19, 20, 114, 118

distorted prices, 27, 28, 112

East African Community (EAC), 129

Economic Commission for Latin America (ECLA), 113, 114, 120

Ecuador, 111

Egypt, 39n3

Ellman, M., 3, 25, 31, 105

El Salvador, 111

European Economic Community (EEC), 79, 124, 165, 166, 167, 168, 170, 171, 172, 173
European Commission, 155, 157, 161

European Currency Unit (ECU), 52

European Investment Bank (EIB), 161, 171

European Parliament, 165, 173n

exchange rate, 25, 28, 38, 51, 64, 65, 67, 74, 116, 119, 122, 136, 138, 139, 140, 147, 154, 177, 180
fixed (or pegged), 3, 10, 16, 24, 25, 31, 32, 38, 45, 47, 48, 49, 53, 54, 175
flexible (or floating), 16, 23, 24, 25, 31, 36, 45, 47, 49, 53, 145, 175
devaluation, 52, 53, 64, 117, 127, 134, 135, 136, 139, 140

exports,
export earnings, 2, 12, 13, 18, 19, 130
purchasing power of export earnings, 7, 18

Felix, D., 125n

Filgueira, C., 115

fiscal policy, 4, 20, 21, 27, 30, 47, 49, 52, 70, 76, 101, 105, 106, 182, 187
budget deficit, 21, 27, 29, 30, 35, 47, 51, 83, 97, 99, 106, 117, 131, 136, 145, 156, 178, 180, 181
public sector borrowing requirements, 30, 101, 122
tax burden, 17, 28, 29, 35, 36, 178

Fischer, S., 101

Fishlow, A., 115

Ford Administration, 50

foreign exchange shortage (constraint) (see balance of payments),

France, 52, 62, 80, 81, 83, 86, 88, 91, 124

Frei Regime, 117

Friedman, M., 24, 41n, 45, 47, 48, 49, 50, 53, 69, 72, 74, 75, 76, 77, 78, 85, 94n, 106, 108

190

Furtado, C., 114

Gabon, 40n
Galbraith, J. K., 69, 86
Garvy, G., 97
Germany, 44,
    Democratic Republic of, 98
    Federal Republic of, 71, 88, 154
Gierek Government, 103
Gilder, G., 89
Giscard d'Estaing Government, 94n
Godley, W., 40n, 41n
gold, 16, 25, 32, 45, 46, 47, 51, 52,
    53, 175, 176
    standard, 4, 44, 119
Great Depression, 4, 8, 84, 103
Greece, 39n
Green, R. H., 148n
Griffith-Jones, S., 97, 118
Group of 24, 157, 173n
Group of 30, 118n
Group of 77, 151, 152, 165
Guatemala, 111
Gutowski, A. (Gutowski-Roth
    Plan), 164, 165, 168, 170,
    172, 173n

Heertje, A., 3, 25, 26, 27, 30, 39
Hill, T. P., 40n
Holsen, J. A., 153
Hong Kong, 39n
Hungary, 20, 97, 98

income distribution, 34, 97, 105,
    114, 115, 142
income policy, 21, 27, 49, 70, 75,
    76, 97, 103
India, 12, 39n, 40n, 162
Indonesia, 12, 39n, 71
inflation,
    effects of, 16, 19, 20, 28-29
    inflationary expectations, 30, 70,
        72, 178, 179, 182
interest rates, 2, 4, 12, 15, 16, 23,
    28, 30, 31, 36, 38, 52, 71, 72,
    73, 74, 75, 77, 105, 123, 135,
    136, 138, 140, 145, 166, 180,
    181, 182

International Bank for
    Reconstruction and
    Development (IBRD, World
    Bank), 39n, 117, 128, 132,
    136, 142, 150, 160, 161, 168
    capital market (Eurodollar
        market), 13, 14, 23, 25, 46,
        106, 152, 153, 158, 161, 163,
        170
    division of labour, 7, 8, 14
    Keynesianism, 14, 15, 39, 149,
        150, 153, 186
    Monetary Fund (IMF), 12, 28,
        32, 33, 34, 36, 39n, 40n, 45,
        46, 111, 112, 118, 127-48,
        156, 157, 158, 160, 164, 168,
        176, 177, 178, 184, 188n
    monetary system, 3, 19, 32, 38,
        45, 65, 175, 176, 177
Israel, 71
Italy, 64, 81, 88

Jamaica, 40n
Jansen, K., 40n, 41n
Japan, 44, 122, 124, 154, 172
Jaruzelski Government, 81
JASPA, 128
Jayawardena, L., 3, 10, 15, 31, 39,
    158, 164, 173n, 186
Jenkins, R., 151
Johnson, H. G., 40n

Kaldor, N., 30, 41n
Kalecki, M., 26, 104
Kania Government, 103
Keller, P. M., 33
Kemp-Roth Bill, 50
Kenya, 39n, 40n
Kerstenetsky, I., 124n
Keynes, J. M., 26, 49, 60, 82, 87,
    103, 106, 151
    Keynesian economic policies, 19,
        20, 21, 22, 23, 37, 38, 48, 49,
        62, 123, 176, 186
    (post) Keynesian economics
        (economists), 1, 3, 20, 21, 50,
        51, 61, 65, 83, 84, 85, 90, 93,
        101, 102, 103, 104, 105, 106,

191

Index

107, 113, 122, 123, 125n
Khan, M. S., 33
Killick, T., 135
Knight, M. D., 33
Krebbs, P., 94n

labour productivity, 2, 8, 9, 17, 116, 123, 178
Laidler, D., 24, 41n
Lawrence, R. Z., 124n
Leijonhufvud, A., 27
Leipziger, D. M., 39n
less developed countries (LDCs), low income countries, 5, 13, 152, 185
  newly industrialised countries (NICs) or major exporters of manufacturers, 7, 9, 33, 35, 111, 185
  primary commodities exporters, 2, 7, 15, 16, 22, 111, 112, 113, 153
Liberia, 40n
Luxemburg, R., 186

McAuley, A., 99
Malaysia, 39n
Mandel, E., 4, 7, 17, 21, 29, 32, 40n, 79
Marx, K., 90
Marxism, marxist theory, 1, 4, 17, 82, 83, 90, 101, 102, 107, 120, 121, 125n, 186
Mexico, 12, 39n, 40n, 80, 111
Minsky, H. P., 103
Mitterrand Government, 52, 62, 90, 91
monetary approach to the balance of payments, 32, 47, 134
  authorities (Central Bank), 30, 45, 46, 47, 65, 69, 70, 71-72, 73, 74, 75, 99, 101, 103, 176, 180
  policy, 4, 29, 30, 36, 43, 47, 48, 49, 51, 52, 53, 72, 73, 75, 76, 81, 96, 97, 99, 100, 101, 102, 103, 104, 105, 107, 117, 118, 176, 179, 180, 181, 182, 187

control of money supply, 24, 25, 31, 45, 94n, 103, 108, 179, 181, 185
definition of money supply, 25, 48, 94n, 103, 179
money and the real economy, 25, 56-57, 96, 100
  stock (supply), 4, 19, 39n, 48, 50, 53, 57, 58, 69, 74, 96, 100, 101, 102, 103, 111, 117, 122, 131, 134, 145, 180
Mongolia, 98
Morgan Guaranty Trust, 156
Mundell, R. A., 3, 16, 17, 19, 25, 30, 31, 38, 47
multinational corporations (MNCs), 23, 34, 67, 81

Nakajima, M., 151, 162, 163
neo-classical economics, 26, 27, 56, 112, 113, 120, 121, 140
  Pareto-optimality, 56
Netherlands, 71, 72, 74, 76, 86
New International Economic Order (NIEO), 149
newly industrialised countries (NICs) (see less developed countries)
Nicaragua, 40n
Nigeria, 39n
Nixon Administration, 50

oil market, 10, 65-66, 163, 166, 170, 172
  price increases, 2, 7, 8, 9, 10, 12, 14, 15, 16, 63, 65-66, 101, 129, 150, 153, 155, 163, 168, 169, 170, 179
Organisation of Economic Cooperation and Development (OECD), 39n, 40n, 94n, 128, 163, 165, 166, 168, 172
Organisation of Petroleum Exporting Countries (OPEC), 14, 65, 66, 150, 153, 154, 155, 158, 160, 163, 164, 165, 166,

167, 168, 169, 170, 171, 172, 173
Ortega Gomez, E., 172

Pakistan, 39n, 40n
Palma, G., 124n
Pareto-optimality (see neo-classical economics)
Peru, 39n, 40n, 111
Phillips-curve, 20, 178
Pinto, A., 113
Podolsky, T. M., 109n
Polak, J. J., 3, 8, 19, 21, 25, 28, 30, 32, 33, 39, 41n, 134, 176
Poland, 12, 31, 81, 98, 99, 105, 106
Portes, R., 100, 109n
Portugal, 39n, 40n, 88, 90
post-Keynesian economics (see Keynes)
Prebish, R., 112, 113, 114, 124n
primary commodity exporters (see less developed countries)
Profits
    profitability (rate of profit), 16, 17, 18, 22, 23, 24, 29, 30, 31, 83, 88, 90, 91, 112, 178
    profit share, 2, 17, 18, 29, 31, 36
public sector borrowing requirement (see Fiscal Policy)

Quadros Government, 116
quantity theory of money, 24, 102

Ramos, S., 125n
Reagan Administration, 50, 54n, 62, 72, 81, 83, 85, 89, 92, 94n
Recycling, 31, 80, 153, 154, 155, 157, 158, 163, 164, 170, 183, 184
Reichman, T. M., 41n
Romania, 12, 31, 98, 105
Rosenberg, S., 40n
Roth, W. (see Gutowski)
Rowthorn, R. E., 17
Russia (see USSR)
Rwegasira, D. G., 148n

Saudi Arabia, 172
Schumpeter, J., 109n
Seers, D., 3, 4, 9, 25, 27, 39, 124n
Sideri, S., 125n
Sierra Leone, 40n
Simatupang, B., 105
Singapore, 39n
Singer, H., 112, 124n
socialist countries (see centrally planned economies)
South Korea, 39n3, 80, 122
Spain, 90
Special Drawing Rights (SDRs), 46, 51, 52, 165, 166, 167, 168, 176, 184
Spraos, J., 124n
Sri Lanka, 39n, 40n, 158
stagnation thesis, 114, 115
Stillson, R. T., 41n
structuralist approach (structuralism), 1, 3, 9, 27, 112, 113, 114, 115, 116, 119, 121, 122, 124n
structuralist vs monetarist debate in Latin America, 27, 110-114, 146
Sudan, 39n, 40n
Sunkel, O., 113
supply-side economics, 30, 48-51, 74-75
Switzerland, 71, 181
Syria, 39n

Tanzania, 15, 18, 28, 34, 39n3, 80, 127-148
tax burden (see fiscal policy)
Temin, P., 39n
terms of trade, 18, 22, 32, 101, 112, 116, 129, 139, 140, 156
Thatcher Government, 62, 83, 85
Tobin, J., 69
Togo, 40n
trade (world trade), 4, 5, 7, 23
trade unions, 17, 30, 71, 76, 83, 86, 101, 102, 105, 123
transfer pricing, 116
Tunisia, 39n
Turkey, 39n, 40n, 90

Index

Uganda, 129
Unemployment, 2, 4, 7, 8, 9, 10, 15,
    16, 19, 21, 25, 29, 48, 49, 50,
    51, 53, 57, 70, 71, 73, 74, 76,
    78, 79, 80, 84, 86, 87, 88, 89,
    92, 101, 104, 119, 121, 122,
    123, 150, 151, 175
Union of Socialist Soviet Republics
    (USSR), 44, 98, 99, 106, 118,
    121
United Kingdom (UK), 4, 35, 55,
    62, 64, 74, 77, 81, 82, 83, 84,
    86, 88, 123
United Nations (UN), 149, 165
    Conference on Trade and
        Development (UNCTAD),
        149, 150, 151
United States of America (USA), 4,
    8, 39n, 40n, 41n, 44, 45, 47,
    48, 49, 50, 55, 62, 63, 71, 72,
    73, 74, 80, 82, 83, 84, 86, 87,
    91, 92, 94n, 113, 122, 123,
    155, 156, 180, 181
Usoskin, V. M., 109n

Van Arkadie, B., 3, 4, 15, 18, 28,
    33, 34, 39, 148n
Venezuela, 39n, 111, 158
Vietnam, 105
Vines, S., 173
Volcker, P. A., 72, 73
Vuskovic, P., 117

Waelbroeck, J. L., 153
wages
    real, 4, 17, 18, 23, 28, 29, 31, 37,
        83, 118, 139, 178
    wage share, 17, 18, 35, 36, 114
Weber, M., 44
Weiskopf, T. E., 40n
Wells, J., 115
Williamson, J., 188n
Witteveen, H. J., 160
World Bank (see IBRD)

Yugoslavia, 39n

Zammit, A., 124n
Zaire, 39n, 40n